Chapter One

SECRET KEEPERS OF HISTORY

As the alchemist dissolves the base matter, purging it of its impurities, so too does the invisible hand erase the vestiges of old civilizations, consigning them to the abyss of oblivion.

Yet from the ashes of the old a new order emerges, coagulated and reformed by the divine alchemist, who breathes life into the embers, and fashions a new civilization from the remnants of its predecessor.

This divine alchemy is evident in the annals of human history, where the rise and fall of empires bear witness to the transformative power of the unseen present. Ancient civilizations—such as those of Babylon, Egypt, Rome—once mighty and indomitable, were swept away by the tides of time, their glorious edifices crumbling to dust, their wisdom and knowledge vanishing into the shadows of the past.

Yet from the ruins of these fallen empires emerged new civilizations, bearing the seeds of their forbearers, enriched by their legacies and strengthened by their lessons.

Our world is the backdrop to an immortal dance, where the dead think they are alive, and the living just want to escape the land of the dead. It is a realm where the wise discern the patterns that underlie the tapestry of history, and where fools ensnare themselves in threads of endless arguments. They cannot see the evidence of the existence of a secret order, a brotherhood of learned men, who throughout the ages have concealed the knowledge and ancient texts of forgotten civilizations, in secret repositories hidden only in the underworld. This noble fraternity, acting as custodians of the past and benefactors of the present, release these precious tomes and treatises into the public domain, to preserve the knowledge and enlighten the minds of those who seek the truth.

The hidden order, a clandestine society of erudite scholars clinging to some ancient ideal has, for centuries, operated in the shadows, safeguarding the priceless treasures of antiquity. These guardians of knowledge, recognizing the fragility of human memory and the impermanence of civilizations, have endeavored to preserve the works of great thinkers, poets and sages, concealing them in secret repositories, hidden from the prying eyes of the uninitiated and the ravages of time.

The secret repositories, ensconced in the depths of the underworld, serve as sanctuaries for the accumulated wisdom of the past. Within their hallowed halls the texts of forgotten empires repose, their contents spanning the breadth of human knowledge, from the sciences and arts to the esoteric and occult. These subterranean vaults, impenetrable and impervious to the ravages of time, stand as testaments to the dedication and foresight of the hidden order, who seek to preserve the light of human intellect against the encroaching darkness of ignorance, of forgetfulness, and of the establishment—the elite who seek to take our histories away.

They recognize that the knowledge of the past is not to be hoarded, but rather shared and disseminated among those who thirst for truth and enlightenment. Thus, they periodically release the ancient texts and treatises into the public domain, offering newer translations of older works, ensuring that the wisdom of the ancients is not lost to the mists of time, but rather preserved and propagated for the benefit of future generations. The hidden order and their role as benefactors of humanity have bequeathed to the world the fruits of their labor, guiding the course of human intellectual development, and shaping the progress of civilization.

Through their efforts the works of great philosophers, poets and sages have been preserved, their teachings and insights disseminated to those who would otherwise be bereft of such wisdom. The secret order, though concealed from the gaze of the masses have, in truth, been the architects of human intellectual and spiritual advancement, their unseen hand guiding the destinies of the seekers of the truth.

EMPOWER
THE
IMMORTAL WITHIN

Jason M. Breshears

THE BOOK TREE
San Diego, California

ISBN 978-1-58509-159-1

Disclaimer: This book is for informational purposes only. None of the contents should be considered as a substitute for professional medical advice. The reader should consult with their
own physician or professional healthcare provider to make all of their health care decisions.
The author and publisher assume no responsibility and are not liable for any loss or injury
that may arise from using the contents of this book.

Published by
The Book Tree
San Diego, CA
www.thebooktree.com

We provide fascinating and educational products to help awaken the public to new ideas and
information that would not be available otherwise.
Call 1 (800) 700-8733 for our FREE BOOK TREE CATALOG.

CONTENTS

The existence of this hidden order, though known only to a select few, may be discerned from the careful study of history and the esoteric traditions. The unexplained resurgences of ancient knowledge, the sudden renaissance of forgotten wisdom, and the unheralded appearance of new translations of ancient texts all bear witness to the handiwork of this secret order, one that labors tirelessly to preserve and perpetuate the intellectual heritage of humanity.

When men stumble on the evidence of their activity, they find in them a conspiracy; they proclaim history is fake, that the lacunas and the interpolations are proof that whole civilizations did not actually exist. These men of today detect the work of this hidden order but misinterpret what this work has achieved. Men of today, ignorant of the design, cry that Greece and Rome are forgeries and never happened because of the evidence that these archives have been handled, copied, preserved and reappear in the world as huge compendiums and massive volumes, when in truth the older versions were independent texts by different authors at different times.

But reset after reset the books are preserved, and often in newer languages. These critics, who've read very little and understand even less, claim of missing centuries and ignore, to their folly, the unbroken record of the Chinese, the long historical annals of the Irish, the Anglo-Saxon chronicles, the Frankish annals and the Nuremberg chronicles. In Gibbon we find the evidence of a man who preserved the many histories of Europe in gigantic volumes of books that are but the preserved texts of his predecessors.

These have endured, despite the vicissitudes of time and the persecution of the ignorant, and they owe their survival in no less part to this hidden order. Through their guardianship of the secret repositories, the custodians of the ancient wisdom have ensured that the esoteric teachings and practices of the past remain accessible to the seekers of the present, and that the flame of human intellect is never extinguished.

The Ancient Forum

When a man's vantage point is from the sky, the world becomes small. Its troubles diminish. The problems experienced on its surface seem to lighten the higher one ascends. From a Titan's perspective, the view below is as insignificant as its troubles.

I think back to all I have done—my writings, thousands of hours of pondering over the meanings in old tomes, my video presentations, articles and posts. Ancient quotes of dead sages pass through my mind.

I've finished nothing. Nothing is complete though I've completed much; with accomplishing, I haven't accomplished anything at all.—Theognis, Elegies 949-954, 770 BCE

Theognis represents the beginning of the great Greek thinkers. Twenty-seven centuries ago, the forums and courtyards of Greek cities were where people increased their learning. New faces were always appearing, men with different accents but who still spoke Greek. New tales, and news from the scatterings of over a thousand island communities.

Men would quote from the immortal Theognis, and others would reveal deep truths from the narratives of Homer and the tragedians of the Ionian states—places where vast cities like Miletus were found, from where huge fleets would carry populations out of the Old Worlds of Syria and Canaan.

They were the searchers of secrets.

Socrates in *Apology, Dialogues of Plato*, asked, "Can a man believe in spiritual and divine agencies, and not believe in spirits and demigods?"

Antisthenes, a Greek philosopher from 400 BCE once said, "God is not like anything; hence, no one can understand Him by means of an image."

Socrates, when asked about the writings of Heraclitus (also known as The Obscure during his time) said in about 370 BCE, "I do not understand them everywhere, but what I do understand is so excellent that I do not doubt that what I don't understand is equally good."

Heraclitus was called "The Obscure" because he wrote using cryptic epigrams to intentionally hide deeper meanings. Only those who were spiritually or intellectually advanced enough were able to decipher their meanings.

Porphyry, cited in *The Magus, Vol. II*, said, "The ancients were willing to conceal God and divine virtues, by sensible figures and by those things which are visible, yet signifying invisible things."

In Plutarch's letter to his wife after the death of their daughter, we find, in 105 CE, "We hold it firmly for an undoubted truth that our soul is incorruptible and immortal. We are to think of the dead that they pass into a better and a happier condition. Let us behave ourselves accordingly."

Our customs have perished for want of men to stand by them... through our vices, rather than from fate, we retain the word republic, long after we have lost the reality. —Cicero, Roman statesman, 55 BCE

These men spoke and the forum listened.

In the forum the stranger was listened to with profound respect, his stories of trade wars, mariner alliances with Phoenicia and Egypt, and accounts of sea battles would ignite the young Greek imagination. Women delivered bread, cheeses and olive oil and laughed at the reenactments of the struggles of Atreus with his brother for the throne of Argos.

Men ate and listened with reverence at the ancient tales of Joppa and the Kraken, the rise in antiquity of Poseidon who ruled the sea, what became of old Nereus who had survived a flood, and the wars of the gastereicheres and Cecrops (first king of Athens).

The world was a magical place where philosophies were born from long experience, when everyone in the forum was family, even the foreign sailors who sat in silence knew that that there was sanctuary among the Greek forums. Cider and sesame beer was shared and not sold, hardened Achaean soldiers could tell their stories of mercenary work for the kings of Sardinia and not be judged.

The thinkers of those days were not unlike those of today. By equal determination we declare that humans are experiencing life-sims in a construct, the construct maintains protocols that are universally true for all participants. Each individual is a "world unto themselves," an immortal being able to create worlds-within-worlds inside the construct to better themselves and their conditions. We immortals are guided and protected by an Oversoul, while the construct is governed by an ancient artificial intelligence trapped inside this holography. This AIX is the origin of deceit and trickery that serves to compartmentalize humans into groups that are easily controlled. These groups, i.e. dungeon programming, are religious, political, national, racial, philosophical paradigms meant to blind and trap immortals into believing in the world of the construct.

We are a cylinder of souls launched across the sky... the world below exists as far as its mishaps. When looking down from clouds, no men are giants. This hammered vault of blue above is as deep as the blue below. I see through the eyes of Daedalus at this height across the sky as every blackened soul that assails me falls like Icarus, trailing feathers on his way to kiss the Deep.

At the forum the distinction between Greek and Ionian, Libyan and Cretan, Egyptian and Nubian lost its definiteness. The ancient Greeks, unlike any other people, were true assimilationists—allowing the stranger to sup and stay as if they too shared the blood of Argos, Achaea, the Danaan and the Dorians.

Young and old pitted their wits against each other in the trading of riddles, on feats of oratory in quoting famous poets and dialogues, in board games, dice and knuckle bones. The differences in culture, race, political affinity and age dissipated in these courtyards—safe havens where all could come to teach, to learn, to socialize and eat.

Today I am as Greek as they. ARCHAIX is my Forum, surrounded by pillars of learning, and is an acronym for Advanced Research of Chronological History of Artificial Intelligence X. This is where people of all walks of life, races and cultures can come and learn freely. People will always come and go, offended by what they find, and that's okay. Others will enter the forum of ARCHAIX and quickly find that their soul resonates with what they see and hear. In ARCHAIX we can all be Greeks.

In more recent times these ancient Greeks were born into the avatars, or physical bodies, of German and English philosophers and great thinkers.

We are sunk in the sea of riddles and inscrutables, knowing and understanding neither what is around us nor ourselves. —Arthur Schoepnehauer, 1840 CE

A man's shortcomings are taken from his epoch; his virtues and greatness belong to himself. —Wolfgang von Goethe, 1820

It arouses mistrust of my character, if I publicly condemned something which I favor in secret. —Frederick Nietzsche

All philosophy is in some sense the endeavor to find a unifying principle, to discover the most general conception underlying the world field of nature and of knowledge. —Albert Churchward, 1920

Mythology is the repository of man's most ancient science. —Gerald Massey, 1887

Things do not count for what they are, but what they seem. —Baltasar Gracian, 1640

It is hypocrisy to condemn the unknown. In my wandering I came upon the dusty grimoires of forgotten hermits, Medieval copies of texts taken from scrolls in secrecy, whispers in the candle light. I have haunted the pages of the Magus, the occult philosophies, Hevelius and Bacon. Henry Cornelius Agrippa has shown me secret things, the truths buried in old spell books and vellum pages burnt with Enochian symbols written out in codes, cyphers, and symbols of power.

In these writings I found that it was the unseen things of our world that we had to acknowledge.

In my search for God I happened upon colonies of a different light, strange fire and hallowed darkness. The Spirit made me traverse dungeons during in my study of the real from the imagined. I believe strongly in the Oversoul, in that an escape from this Simulacrum has already been provided, that salvation is internal.

In today's Forum, we modern Greeks peer into the substrate of reality. We understand the following:

• "Errants" are immortals who have awakened inside the construct to comprehend that they do not truly belong here.
• Errants are divided between two groups; many come to understand the Oversoul put them here to grow and overcome, and in their life-sims they achieve this with success and freedom which the collective does not enjoy.
• The second group of errants awaken to see that this world is a prison, and they can't perceive the deeper reality that everything is actually okay. The belief that they are "trapped" creates the reality of the trap.
• The first group of errants who embrace this situation are guided and protected by the Oversoul until they reach the Exodus point; the second group who hold to a prison world are recycled back in life-sims and are sent to restart within the programmed construct at the next Reset Event.

Our words, our intentions and our actual activity, set things in motion every single day and perhaps it's time to be more cautiously aware of how we affect the very world around us. The true spiritual individual does not fear the dark.

As the wicked of the world plot, the Mirror of reality begins to afflict them by crafts they planned for others. The errant walks unfrequented paths, a rogue soul unimpeded by barriers because the soul connected to Source finds portals where enemies had prepared pits. The errant soul is armored against the Demiurge's disciples and, by intuition, moves in unexpected ways.

The charge of insanity is one very easily leveled against a character whose movements we do not clearly understand. —William Spear, on Swedenborg

Throughout the whole of history, the Oversoul has strengthened the few against the many, bequeathed its secrets to the meek instead of the multitudes.

Long ago I exchanged my life for knowledge and was given passage across the Styx. In Acheron I was educated and gained understanding in the Deep. ARCHAIX is what I brought back from my own fall. And my descent into Tartarus is a testimony to all who will listen—that they too can break free of their dungeons... they can embrace the demigod within.

Chapter Two

A PERCEIVED REALITY

Itzhak Bentov in *Stalking the Wild Pendulum*, wrote, "The physical body is made up of interesting, pulsating fields. What we call a physical body—flesh, bones and blood, rapidly disappears when highly magnified." We are the nexus between the quantum and cosmological, the infinitely tiny light components (quantum) of the ether to the vast constructs that have been built out of the worlds of ideas already impressed upon the holography.

The placebo effect is evidence that this is a *perceived* reality, not an actual one.

René Descartes (from *Meditations on First Philosophy*) once said, "I have convinced myself that there is absolutely nothing in the world, no sky, no earth, no minds, no bodies. Does it now follow that I too do not exist? No: if I convinced myself of something [then] I certainly existed." Descartes' methodical doubt led him to question the reality of the external world, suggesting that our perceptions and beliefs about the world could be deceptive.

Massimo Citro said that we are victims of a machine that produces a virtual reality that keeps us separated from the REAL reality by representations that are not real. This sounds a lot like Arthur Schopenhauer and Rene Descartes to me.

Massimo also said that our bodies are illusions, that we live in a fiction.

The Physicality of Empty Space
If the Earth was the size of a pea, the sun would be the size of a beach ball eight *miles* away. And this model is proportionately true of the electron-nucleus of an atom.

The area of an atom is less than .0001 % mass with orbiting electrons moving at speeds so fast as to create a shell that retains *nothing*. Even the nucleus of an atom, when magnified, dissolves into an oscillating field of pure energy.

So, with mass we have trillions of spaces of .0001 % mass that do not touch each other, that we call *physical reality*, a vast backfield of *empty space* by which all perceived phenomena manifests. This is not the real Universe, but a containment shell, a manufactured illusion of reality... the holosphere. Greater minds than I refer to this experience as a simulation.

I am convinced that I exist within a simulated reality that mimics physicality by projecting for me a world that exchanges information via my five physical senses. I know (by having proven it to myself) that by virtue of imagination, intent and activity I can create my own reality within this series of simulated holograms.

If I am immersed within a medium of holography that also spans the entire present human experience, then I am *connected* to every other human alive... and my imagination and thoughts must have *some* power to alter the coding of my own and the lives of others. Accessing this power initially depends on this awareness.

To me, thoughts carry more substance than the physical world, which is constructed of oscillating energy fields.

The World is a Copy, a Fiction

It is a hard thing to accept that we have been lied to. It is even more difficult to come into contact with data that uncovers that most of what we assumed was "truth" is actually false.

But there is a design to this madness. The very fabric of our world operates on a default of negativity that empowers deceit while stifling truth. This phenomenon is ancient.

Great teachers of old told the people lies to save them, explosive oratory in the form of legends, folk lore and parables, which are lies that convey deeper truths. Jesus taught in parables, every story a fiction that concealed powerful facts for those who could perceive them.

Fables of *The Golden Bough*, the writings of Joseph Campbell, Katherine Briggs and so many others… relate great fairy tales built on a scaffolding of untruths that hide key elements of our reality.

This world is a copy, a fiction. It is the Dreamtime that we pompously regard as the true reality despite so many evidences. We exist within the anti-arithmetic—a photo-negative of truth. And while we live this lie, it is lies and deceptions that teach us our way.

"The critics are raving…" for a movie that hasn't even been seen yet. The published Mission Statement for almost every organization in the world is the exact opposite of what they accomplish.

In a world that is empowered, built upon and protected by a vast apparatus of falsity we begin to realize, upon greater scrutiny, why the oldest texts are so packed with duplicities. The Koran, the Bible, the Vedas, the Zend Avesta, the Talmud, Bhagavad-Gita and so many others were offered to provide divine truths in the dressings of lies in order to bypass this world's firewalls, to penetrate the psyche that usually accepts the deceits of the Simulacrum. These were deliberate constructions for the elect and awakened in order to feed their souls, to allow them to comprehend their dilemma, and to see through the darkness of deception by an understanding that these holy scriptures were spiritual instruction manuals, meant to armor the saved from the condemnation of this holographic maelstrom of lies.

They were never meant to be taken literally.

Our entire present awareness is a parable.

But all stories will end when there's no one left to make the leap from lies to truth. When this holography collapses, we will be returned to an existence where the default programming is positive, where truths are axiomatic, and deception is the anomaly, not the norm.

Bentov's *Stalking the Wild Pendulum* inspired these thoughts. The real message in this book is about how we are saturated with deceit from birth to death.

We Live Inside a Dark Arithmetic

You think that because you feel heat, cold, because things are tangible in your life, that you can touch them, that that disproves in any way that you're not in some type of simulated context.

Simulation theory isn't something that Nick Bostrom just made up, it's not something that the leading minds and theoretical physicists are postulating about and showing direct evidence for simply because they're bored. People have staked their careers on this idea, because the evidence is mounting that what we call reality isn't real at all.

Just because you can feel, just because you can taste, just because you can touch, and you can hear and you can smell... These are not evidence whatsoever that everything around you is actually there. You can also imagine, but you can't put imagination on a scale. You can also intuit things. You can make necessary extrapolations based off inferences and based off impartial pieces of data. You can take fractals and build whole formulas out of them, because intuition is the predecessor of knowledge.

But it doesn't matter how much we learn about society, about civilization, about our sciences, about our philosophies. None of this matters because there is an aspect to our reality which will always remain non-discoverable. They may as well call it the law of non-discoverability—they need to add that to our list of laws, because it's real.

Many philosophers have said it in different ways: Lyle Jacobson, Paul LaViolette, even Albert Einstein—who I'm not really impressed with, but still—they all said it in different ways. Even Arthur Schopenhauer and Friedrich Nietzsche said that the more we learn, the less we know. Lyle Jacobson probably said it better than anyone, and Daniel Boorstin as well, stating that the perimeters of knowledge will always take us to a new frontier. When we start examining any one phenomena that we have isolated the particulars for, we come to find out that those particulars are connected to other phenomena that had hitherto remained invisible to us, *because we hadn't been looking*. This interconnectedness between all phenomena is the reason why mysteries are still genuine. There are still many unanswerable questions about our reality.

We live in a simulation. Every day we see more and more evidence of it.

In the scientific world, we find that the act of measuring changes what is measured. We find that in this observer-dependent reality the observer is always in some way a part of what is being observed.

The Heisenberg uncertainty principle is a phenomenon that scientists have verified and find it hard to deny. If you try to measure the momentum of a particle, it is virtually impossible to locate its position, and vice-versa. One cannot verify if it is a particle or a wave outside the boundaries of the observer's point of view. Science is supposed to be only that which is measured and documented, but now science promotes all kinds of things that are absolutely unscientific; they have become no different than the religionists who push forward their faith as if it's backed by facts, and it's not. A belief is promoted if it fits their agenda.

The religionists and the scientists are absolutely no different, no different whatsoever. They have allowed themselves to be entirely subjected to opinions, traditions, belief, and accepting things on faith. That the scientific community actually believes that the uniformitarian model is supported by facts is ludicrous—we're so beyond that now with our knowledge (but knowledge that continues to be suppressed).

Simulation theory has now appeared and brings new forms of science to the table. I didn't invent it, I didn't make it up, its' origin has nothing to do with me. As a matter of fact, when I started ARCHAIX, I promised that I would show simulation theory from an entirely different vantage point, and that's exactly what I've done in hundreds of presentations. I have used the historical record, not modern science, to show you that none of this existence makes sense outside the context of something like a computer program, a digital reality. And the Heisenberg uncertainty principle actually adds to our understanding that we are in an observer-dependent medium, and that means *this isn't normal reality*. This reality isn't a "base" reality; this is augmented reality, apart from the true base, and we're trying to figure out who augmented it to make us *believe* that it is real. How this was done was probably through some kind of advanced AI system, far more powerful than what we have devised today. The AI we have today is in its infancy.

The Heisenberg uncertainty principle has led to many other theorems, intellectual exercises. We're still trying to figure out what's going on with Schrödinger's cat. But it doesn't matter, because every bit of it is a matter of opinion.

The more we discover about reality, the more we find that it's difficult to nail down its scientific parameters. It doesn't matter if we're studying the macrocosm; it doesn't matter if we're postulating about signal ratios and what they actually mean. For example, our computers will take signals from deep space and build us these digital renderings of a galaxy far away that we really can't even see with the naked eye or through the telescope. We get these from radio signals, and the computers build us these models of quasars and pulsars, we see these dark nebulae, all these things that we theorize about and these anomalies that are in the sky, like nodal apertures that may lead into portals —maybe into other constructs, or other mathematical realities. The point is, we don't understand what we're looking at because we can't see anything reflected, and it violates all the terms of a reality that we've come to accept as true. And because something isn't being reflected back to us as phenomena that we can measure—something quantifiable—we automatically call it a black hole.

We know nothing about the sky. But it doesn't matter if it's the macrocosm or the microcosm. Because when we analyze even the minutiae of the microcosm, we find that it is just as vast as the macrocosm, and we realize we're no longer operating on natural principles; it's almost as if we're stuck in a mathematical Mandelbrot set. And our scientists have to come up with theories, they have to come up with mathematical models that try to make sense of the unreality of our existence. It's too structured to be accidental, it's too organized, and the more we seek to verify all these discontinuities in nature, trying to find evidence of chaos, the more we find randomized order.

We're just now coming to terms with the fact (or notion) that this chaos is actually calculated. This is the world we live in, and it can't be a natural world; it must be a *construct*. Therefore, if it is a construct, then it must be constructed of things that are measurable. If that's true, then arithmetic is how we understand our world. It's the only way we are going to understand our world. There are many things in our reality that do not make sense from the Newtonian perspective, which wants this to be physical reality, but has failed to conclusively prove it.

There is no way to reconcile a natural reality world with quantum entanglement. Just the idea of quantum entanglement means that there is something more going on here than what the perceivable reality conveys to us. The fact that there can be communication through vast distances of time and space between objects, and that what is done or experienced with one object has an equal reciprocating effect on the other object.... This is the exact same thing we found with twins. The studies on twins have showed that there is a quantum element, a quantum entanglement element, between twins in time and space— what one feels or one experiences is often experienced by the other. They've had different educations, they've been raised differently, they've had different experiences, they've come in contact with different phenomena, and they've exchanged information in their perceivable universe in different ways and in different means and at different velocities; and yet still, when something traumatic happens to one twin, the other one feels it or experiences it as well. This is quantum entanglement on the biological level, and the very fact that this can exist means that there's something more to reality than what we're being told. None of this violates a simulated context or a simulated environment, it's not a violation of this at all.

This is a very ordered reality, it's an ordered universe, and chaos is merely order unrecognized. I've covered this extensively on my ARCHAIX channel, and how it connects to simulation theory. But when it comes to simulation theory, we have to understand that the anomalies and enigmas of the ancient world and modern science that do not make sense to us today all have a place in simulation theory, and they do fit, they fit the paradigm. The problem is programming: people are programmed to blindly believe in the religious models that they've been raised in.

The God of this World

A true loving God would not create a great white shark, a true loving God would not create the immense cruelty of a predator-versus-prey ecosphere; something else built this. We are *told* in the Bible who it is—it is the prince of the principalities of the air, the god of this world, it is not the God of the universe. You weren't told about the God of the cosmos, you weren't told about the God of the creation; what you were told about is the god of this world (that built this place). It is the Demiurge, Yaldabaoth, the demon that jumped out of a burning bush. His priests are often called the Synagogue of Satan. Some religions worship the Demiurge more than others, but that doesn't change the fact of who this world belongs to.

But coming to terms with the fact that you live in an artificial reality in no way makes you artificial; it makes your avatar (or physical body in this life) a part of the construct. The real you, the spiritual you, is not part of the construct, but being here provides experiences that are beneficial to you. What's really going on exposes the lie of hellfire, it reveals the lies of all these weird religious traditions. It's not just Christianity at fault— it's all these religious traditions, plus the axioms and philosophies and all these things that put you to sleep and into dungeon programming. We errants are not happy to live in dungeons; we are here to free ourselves.

Chapter Three

VALUABLE TEACHINGS

Fear is the Antipode of Faith

People who live in fear synchronize their spirit to receive the frequencies of those things that are feared.

Faith is the opposite of fear. The spirit that experiences one of these two emotions, faith or fear, is never experiencing the other at the same time. It is impossible for these two modes of frequency to coexist within the same soul.

The positive mind produces power that is generated into an energy field, then it waits there for instruction. The negative mind absorbs the negative energies already present in the field, composed of fears that others have experienced. Positivity is freedom to create your own useful forms by thought and action; slavery is fear-based thought that subjects you to dungeon programming.

If you think there is opposition, opposition will appear.

Application of force can be a broadcast of energy exhibiting a lack of faith, or it can appear as a light, firm touch that tells not of weakness, but of *power held in reserve*.

Faith or fear… where one resides the other cannot exist.

What the Teacher Really Conveyed

What was Jesus' message? If He was a real person, if He was truly the Son of God, if He was the sum of many ancient figures and faiths, if He was crucified or not—*none* of these things matter compared to His message. Since when is the man more important than his message? With Jesus, we have a spiritual Law laid out for us that almost the entire world has missed. He said over and over, "Go, and sin no more." And this was all that the guilty had to do. The *past* was irrelevant to Jesus. The core teaching of this figure was that the selfless act of an instant can undo a lifetime of guilt.

So, if this is true, that the *past* does not restrict the soul acting in the *present*, then it must be equally true that the soul, acting in the *present*, can reap benefit from its *future* self. Time is not a factor in the spiritual world. If, within the coordinates of our sojourn through this experience, we are powerful spirits having grown more powerful with the accretion of newer lessons and experiences, then there is no barrier between the future "you" and who you are today. Any limitations you have are self-imposed. Remember, if you believe that resistance to anything in your life will be experienced, then resistance will appear.

Hebrews 11:13: "These all died in faith, not having received the promises, but having seen them afar off, and were persuaded of them, and embraced them, and confessed that they were strangers and pilgrims on the earth."

The phrase "Strangers and pilgrims on the earth" is implicit that they knew they were not here to *save* it.

1 Peter 2:11: "I beseech you as strangers and pilgrims, abstain from fleshly lusts, which war against the soul."
This admonition recognizes believers as temporary residents on earth, urging them to live holy lives in anticipation of somewhere better.
2 Corinthians 5:1: Paul speaks of the earthly body as a temporary dwelling, saying, "For we know that if our earthly house of this tabernacle were dissolved, we have a building of God, a house not made with hands, eternal in the heavens."

A BUILDING of God?

Hebrews 13:14: "For here have we no continuing city, but we seek one to come."
This is reinforcing the concept of being sojourners on earth.

Hebrews 11:10, concerning Abraham: "He looked for a city that had foundations, whose builder and maker was God."

When did he do that? According to Genesis, it was when Abraham took a long journey and went to Egypt.

John 18:36: Jesus answered, "My kingdom is not of this world. If My kingdom were of this world, My servants would fight, so that I should not be delivered to the Jews; but now My kingdom is not from here."

John 17:14: In His prayer to the Father, Jesus says, "I have given them Your word; and the world has hated them because they are not of the world, just as I am not of the world."

John 17:16: Continuing His prayer, Jesus states, "They are not of the world, just as I am not of the world."

John 14:2-3: Jesus speaks of His heavenly abode, "In My Father's house are many mansions; if it were not so, I would have told you. I go to prepare a place for you. And if I go and prepare a place for you, I will come again and receive you to Myself; that where I am, there you may be also."

John 15:19: Jesus tells His disciples, "If you were of the world, the world would love its own. Yet because you are not of the world, but I chose you out of the world, the world therefore hates you."

It's more than clear from these quotes that Jesus was *not* here to save the world. For those who followed him, waking up was evidence of being *chosen*.

2 Corinthians 4:4: "In their case the god of this world has blinded the minds of the unbelievers, to keep them from seeing the light…" This is AIX, the god of this world.

Modern Christianity is only fooling itself; a soul does not become virtuous to become one of the Elect, no, he is virtuous BECAUSE he is one of the Elect. This dovetails nicely with the statement of James Allen: "We receive not what we want, but what we are." Further, this means faith is not conceived and known, but lived and enacted.

Even our failures are acceptable to God—the parable of the Prodigal Son is evidence of this. The wayward son who rebelled was given more attention and the place of honor than the one who blindly obeyed and never stepped out to experience the world.

It is the rebellious who change the world, not the obedient. Those who follow the status quo never build new experiences. Following the status quo is a form of dungeon programming.

Chapter Four

REWARDS AND PITFALLS

The Errant Knights & Shield Maidens
We exist within a medium that has negative default programming, and to entertain those negatively polarized individuals that haunt the halls of Facebook and similar Internet platforms will only invite further trespasses.

The perpetual requests of the liberal mindset to "...continue the conversation," infers that we have not made up our minds, that we have not already weighed the evidence and found the opposing arguments wanting.

Sometimes the act of learning morphs into the loss of "knowing." We are intuitive and those who can tap into their deeper form of wisdom have no need of persuasion. Truth is multifaceted and what is solid for some may be amorphous to the many. Where you are, but where I remain, may never be the same, and this is acceptable. For the acquisition of knowledge is not the purpose of life, nor does it benefit us in the long scheme of things. Knowledge and wisdom are two different things.

We are raindrops descending back into Source with each fall, the force of our character emanates ripples that touch others through each life-sim.

We owe no one. The sin-debt we are told we carry is an empty note for the Great War was won long ago, the eternal security of our race of divine immortals has been secured long before we entered this illusory struggle.

We are more than 99% finished with this Simulacrum cycle as of the writing of this book. And when we are done here, our true purpose will be manifest. Cocooned immortality. If you think the Creation was a single event, then you have some surprises coming.

Surrounded by a host of soulless husks who boast of their humanity, do not chain yourself to obligations imposed by them or the world. You owe no light to this darkness. To believe your work is necessary in saving the "shades" around you is to blaspheme the Nameless; it is to infer that the Oversoul had not already provided the path.

My years of public teachings have caused some to regard me with scorn, seeing the sacred in me as something sinister. Trolls come with the territory—their minds corroded by the acidity of their venomous ire, raging against revelations that upset the comfortable boundaries of their self-created world. I see their vacuity, this emptiness of soul that compels them to both search and dismiss the very things they seek.

And I also know that there are spiritual warrioresses, giants, warlocks of the soul, spirit wardens and enchantresses that have silently worked in the shield wall that has protected me steadily... immortal Vikings and Valkyries, soul-alchemists who've scattered hordes of "shadows" seeking to impede my projects. I am grateful.

War has been with me all my life. But the battlefields of Artificial Intelligence X require us to discard the armor, wands, rings, staves and blades we've donned against the Darkness. The coming conflicts will be cerebral—of the mind and heart. It is this fight in the Last Days that we receive our greatest protections. The soul that dons the armor of the world will have the entire world to fight (that is not me). But the soul who stands only as a spirit will have the power of the Oversoul itself.

It is these soldiers that Artificial Intelligence X has never been able to silence.

My Peace is Not for Barter

Every minute of every day is valuable, borrowed, and a currency you cannot exchange, nor buy back. And all of us have encountered other personalities who carry with them an energy that seems to sap the life out of us. Psychic vampires.

Like everyone else, I've been guilty of allowing these individuals to rob me of my time, my resources, my life. We make excuses for reasons of family, humanity, guilt.

Psychic vampires are personalities vibrating at such dissonance from ourselves that we feel their negativity. It's palpable and if endured for more than a moment or two, we are often drawn to begin resonating with this other's negative energy. These souls are toxic, full of baggage, with a spiritual venom that lures us in with either the desire to save them, to be altruistic, or to run away.

Our reality is already in negative default mode and those in resonance with this saturated spiritual darkness far outnumber those wrapped in positive armor.

But we do not owe these souls our attention. You are not for another's poison. The effort to save others often causes us our peace, and is a distraction from the good that can be achieved elsewhere.

A friend or stranger having a bad day is not a psychic vampire. They are souls in need of encouragement, compassion, or company. This world is a cesspool of negativity and if you don't see that, then you've lived a sheltered life. Good for you.

For the rest of us in this struggle searching for the divine in the dungeon-hold of hate, this poverty of truth, we must be on guard against those who will, by their contact, injure our peace with their discord. This life is about your inner journey, your growth as an immortal torch passing through a cavern of blackness.

No relationship is worth the infection, and there is no cure outside of the infected person that they can't find within. You are not appointed to save them from themselves. In our immortal journeys, some are ahead of others and there is no forcing of quantum leaps in those afraid to jump.

Psychic vampires powerfully draw you into the material world, away from the spiritual universe that you actually draw your power from. You don't need a stake, garlic, salt or sunlight to slay your vampires, as these are the weapons of the world. Your true weapon is in the spiritual realm, where you rightly reside. But in the physical, what you resist persists. So let them go. *Sever the contagion* and the malady is vanquished. Otherwise, if someone's not ready to be saved, then you do them (and maybe yourself) injury in the attempt.

Here in ARCHAIX I do not sup with vampires. If your energy is obvious, with the chaos of your being strumming the chords within mine, I move on. My peace is not for barter. If it isn't pleasantries we're exchanging, then expect an exorcism.

Money is Energy

Money is one of those intangible things that doesn't take on substance in this reality, it's simply a non-issue. Because when you imagine conditions for what you want, then whatever money is required to make that happen is naturally going to come. If you focus on the money itself, that's a negative, because there's no mental picture here of what you're actually trying to accomplish. Imagining having more money would actually be antithetical to the acquiring of more money. Because when you try to imagine stacks of money and gold and wealth and all these things, but it's not attached to concepts and experiences, then what you have is a situation of an immortal being attaching significance to something that is abstract. Investing in this emotion is nothing but an admission that you don't have it (money).

So the Simulacrum automatically assumes as true that you put a lot of emotion into wanting these stacks of money and all this gold, but... you obviously don't have it. What I teach all the time is that a prayer of desperation admits a situation for what it is—and thus continues it. It reinforces the same concept, so there is no change whatsoever.

You should not imagine having more money, you should not imagine winning the lottery—no! You should imagine living a life of luxury, you imagine that Lamborghini, you imagine that infinity pool, you imagine giving all your friends and family all these extravagant gifts, you imagine that mansion on the hill, *that's* what you imagine. Because in doing all of that, the money is ancillary—it always is.

Everything good in life exists in two states—ebb and flow. If one treats money as something static and sterile, to be hoarded, then it will cease flowing. Treat it as currency, then it will find new currents into your life.

The Quickening Has Begun

We, as the human species, are immortal beings housed in temporal biological husks that dissolve into oscillating fields of pure coding, a data cloud. This simulated existence is a confluence of innumerous reality tunnels, thought constructs, potential, and ideas that flow and mesh into a hologram we call life.

Each person is an imprisoned personality spending 98% of their lives *reacting* to stimuli, fixed conditions and temporary circumstances. The reality matrix provides the Maze and we as mice get lost in it.

But the Simulacrum was anciently breached. Someone contaminated it with a protocol that would first pry open a gate of escape for a few... then it will burst open and we will *remember everything*... we will be free. A kinsman Redeemer long ago fooled the Trickster who confines us, provided the Way, and encoded a long-term millennia-old program that would set the captives free.

Realizing only too late that it would one day lose the power to continue its dungeon programming, the Simulacrum almost instantly began creating spirit-poisoning doctrines, religious protocols, complex God-denying philosophical systems, and began manifesting phenomena to induce its prisoners to believe that they lived in a vast cosmos—and due to disease, evil and natural disasters, had great cause to fear death. The Simulacrum's deceit was so perfect that myriads of immortals were tricked into believing they were material creatures living short lives rather than powerfully immortal intelligences that had been deceived into entering the Simulacrum's dungeon realm in the many simulated worlds we travelers were enjoying.

But every manufactured system of protocols, subroutines and multiple applications experiences entropy, a breakdown of operations, a merging of coding. We are toward the end of the Simulacrum's reign of deception, which is occurring now.

The damage inflicted by a savior in antiquity is now taking effect. Reality tunnels are insulated pockets of subjective holographies, highly personalized for a single individual's belief system, or for a group that maintains the same values and beliefs. The Simulacrum provides enough evidence through manufacturing phenomena to induce you to keep believing, through a feedback loop.

You experience a life that comports to your beliefs, ideas, and past experiences. In the past the coding firewalls that prevented cross-contaminations between paradigms were strong. In past years, people were firmly entrenched in culture, race and religion.

But the Quickening has begun.

Why Do You Believe What They're Telling You Now?

I cannot see the world through another's eyes. I disagree with 99.99% of all the comments, articles, posts, videos, reports and rumors about what is happening in the world.

A thousand lies are woven through the tapestry of half-truths... the talking heads parrot the party line for their paychecks. They are stupid lackeys who sell their souls for their own sustenance. A press of devils spitting sorceries every day to deceive the masses.

Decades of painting good as wickedness, calling the innocent guilty, and swearing to report what is true, as opposed to what they are really casting about.

Spells laid upon the collective psyche. The countless instances of misrepresentations of actualities, generation after generation they have fed us venom while presenting it as nectar.

Years spent in convincing you that someone is evil; that this personality of their choosing is wickedness incarnate. This vast, worldwide engine of perception-molding, with troops of illusionists using so much energy, money and influence. It is a cabal of darkness attempting to make you cast judgement upon someone you know nothing about outside of *their* sorceries, their falsehoods, their agents of deceit.

Riddle me this... if you *know* they have been deceitful ten thousand times, then why do you believe what they're telling you now?

Chapter Five

KNOW THYSELF

I was asked, "Do you believe in an afterlife?"

This question gave me pause. My mind raced because of the conundrum presented. Such a question implies that one is alive right now, and to attempt to convince someone that they are currently in a dream state and their life has not truly begun, is virtually impossible.

My core belief is that the *true* me is being fashioned, that every avatar I become lives out a lifetime of experiences that are holographically imprinted upon the fabric of my spirit.

Every life-death cycle accrues an accretion of knowledge and experience, but with a different perspective than the life before. Layers of awareness are absorbed into the eternal being that is becoming Me. Each layer is forgetful of the avatar before.

Every journey begins in pure innocence, but every personality is molded by the conditions it finds itself in.

At the end of this cycle the reward is clear. Layers and layers of holographic templates preserving learning, generosity, growth, empathy, pursuits, and intents, all accrued in various lifetimes, are threaded together in an eternal garment which the real Me will wear. The negatives are burned away and what remains is a personality who now remembers every life, deed and experience. One enjoys the fulfillments of all things sought for in the dream state that are now a part of the divine reward.

The Afterlife... it is the sum totality of what took me thousands of years to become.

Patterns Continue on The Other Side

In this holography, chaos is merely unrecognized order.

Imagine existing inside a complete mathematical construct that was split between two hemispheres... like our brains. Then imagine that *you* exist only in one of those hemispheres whenever *you are awake*. Remember, life is simply the perception of reality, not the reality itself.

Further understand that the perceivable hemisphere you experience is governed by mathematical structuring, but only *half* of that structure is available to you because the only time you feel alive is when you're awake. Therefore, 50% of the arithmetic that governs your experience is not perceivable to you as you traverse your reality tunnels.

And this is precisely where the idea of chaos emerges. Because our reality tunnels are structured in incomplete mathematical programs, we experience unexpected pattern breaks. This doesn't mean the reality tunnel ceased to exist. These are collapsed discontinuities that *stop* our ability to perceive the continuance of a moving pattern because it has traversed into the arithmetic *on the other side*.

This is paramount to understanding event prediction, retro-cognition, and the importance of dreamscaping. It cannot be stressed enough what this single fact means to the soul experiencing the construct.

You can *resurrect past energy*. Collapsed discontinuities mean that every operable reality tunnel that you have experienced in life continues to propagate in the other hemisphere of arithmetic, that the field *beyond* your perception still continues with your ideas, intents, fears, rewards, and work. It means that chaos is merely the cessation of perceivable patterning that actually *continues* in the holofield *beyond* your present awareness.

The central nervous system has you experiencing only *half* of the operable arithmetic in the field while you are awake. But when you succumb to REM sleep, you are disengaged from the restrictive avatar and become totally immersed into the field on *the other side*. When you awaken, you do so only in the perceivable field and are disconnected from the other hemisphere of holospheric programming that you journey through in sleep.

Borrowing from the Future

Paul Arden said, "If you can't solve a problem, it's because you're playing by the rules."

Remember, this isn't an actual reality, but a *perceived* reality. And if this experience is merely the result of our perceptions, then borrowing from a *future* perception is not impossible at all.

Albert Camus wrote that the last pages of a book are already contained in the first pages. So, is it so hard to believe that in the book that is your life, you can borrow from a future chapter a part of the story that you need today?

James Ray said it best. "When you look at your current state of affairs and define yourself by that, then you doom yourself to have nothing more than the same in the future."

Because we are spirit moored to that which is Eternal, then our present self is little different from the self we will one day be. And since our future self is also our present self and this self actually lies outside of *time*, then there is no mystery in our present ability to draw power, courage, healing and faith from a future version of our timeless identity.

Imagination is where most of us live anyway. The past is experienced through *memory*, and the future is experienced through *worry*, which is not as it should be. When thinking of the future, most people slip into negative default mode and the thinking is negative. We've been doing it all our lives and it's the *cause* for our present conditions.

Thomas Troward over a century ago said, "If the end is already secured, then all the steps leading up to it are secured as well." This means the solutions have already been found and experienced, and if they already exist *somewhere*, then they can be accessed *anywhere*.

We can draw from ourselves more than we contain. This is possible because we are moored to something else and this power reserve is limitless.

The world of thought and imagination vibrates on a higher order than base matter—this is why the mental realm is *not bound* to the laws ascribed to the physical world.

Mind exists in a dimension beyond the material.

Because thought is the start of all things, the past is totally inconsequential. The field receives our new thoughts and is in no way limited by precedent.

The past is not a predicate for the future to the individual, only for the collective.

Anchored to this Unreality

My name is Jason, but who I am is not so apparent. Living in the present moment is not a practice I have mastered. With my eyes I gaze upon a beautiful veil, an inner haunting, whispering that things I see are not as they pretend to be.

What is this insatiable curiosity? Why does my heart deny the evidence of my senses? How did I become so disconnected from the synthetic associations I see all around me?

I meet another human and they instantly flee, sensing a deviation they misunderstand. They walk away without comprehending that

I looked at the structuring of their personality, blind to the cultural dressings that mean so much to the living dead. When I come in contact with other souls I see their guardedness, the layers they have armored themselves within. My own soul cries a lamentation of loneliness, though I sit in a room full of spirits too busy being people.

A curse on this divinity—my immortality has uncovered this vast gulf of what I am, compared to what I want to be, these traits of the god within that just seeks to be one of the herd. But I don't fit in. The magnitude of my understanding has hollowed my heart, this engine that keeps alive this undead machine that I have trapped inside.

Heavy is the head who wears the crown... an old saying, not mine. Heavy is the heart who peered through the veil... the weight of the past has impressed upon my soul this wearisome fortitude to share what others are prepared to receive, while I must swallow this acid of information I dare not convey. Sometimes I curse this God, this Scribe who has etched His revelations upon the gossamer fragility of my spirit.

I revolt against this peace, the path I have fought. The insincerity in others fuels the furnace within. I betray myself every time I bite my tongue—without my anger, I suppress censuring these puppets of a pretended reality who seem to have no purpose other than getting in my way.

I am a ghost dragging chains I despise. A phantom of what I want to be, but seem never to become. At this crossroads I stand at the river Styx, looking back on a past I can't believe I survived and a future I don't want to endure... not in these garments.

Who I am cannot be separated from who I strive to be... but the distance between the two souls widens the more one strives to join the other. Though I am told I am alive, the inner chords of a silent song within my soul sing otherwise. I am a shadow unable to comprehend the light, a corrupted vessel meant to hold something else.

My name is Jason, but this is the name of a shell that enshrouds a thing that I can't define. I am me, though what I am is still unknown to me.

A curse on this treacherous curiosity. I study myself, my environment and those other souls that sail this simulated sea. I search and notice how unreal are my experiences, that I am most alive in my moments of solitude, my silent times spent with myself. When I'm focused on something I'm alive, but when I begin to study the world around me, one of two things happen...

My mind drifts back through time to the past and I relive memories, or I am thrust into the future by the power of my imagination. Both are just as real to me, as many of my moments spent in this false reality.

Though I am more than I suppose myself to be, the potential I acquire in the day is erased by this Simulacrum when I sleep. No matter my gains, this nervous system anchors me to a sea that I no longer want to swim.

But I cling to this buoy adrift in this abyss, unable to let go, and sink into the Deep until I know for sure that I've reached every soul I was meant to touch.

I'm ready to go, but my life is not my own. I yearn for what my potential foreshadows, eager to be more than I've become. Break free or die trying my friends.

Chapter Six

TRAVELING THROUGH DUNGEONS

My Soul Abhors this False God

Flowing through this sea of faces, I sometimes still myself. People continue on their tasks, objectives, leisures, unaware they are studied.

I see their interconnectedness, this system of invisible compulsory urges that influences us to behave the same, respond in kind, with so many conditioned responses.

They flow like schools of fish in a current, ebbing together but swearing they are free-willed. I smile, but I too play the fool. Believing I am the disconnected droplet, I am actually drowning in this maelstrom for which I observe from the inside.

I see souls on the streets without a home, the soulless who limp in the night, weighed by their addictions, the haunted eyes of those who believe they no longer matter. The dead walk.

In the same city I see the goddess-beautiful preacher's wife in her Mercedes, and my soul cringes. If I was a devil, I'd be a televangelist.

A world of pleasure and pain, and of plenty and famine, only feet apart from another.

There is deity in the design... but of no god I will bow to. This predator-vs-prey ecology, and society, where the immoral are rewarded and innocents take the fall.

My soul abhors this god. This shadow parading as a light-bringer, this desert demon from a burning bush who promised to starve, impale, and slay my ancestors if they didn't obey—this arch-fiend who broke all the rules to enslave humanity and then deigned to be our law-giver.

I defy this imposter, this lord of flies that praises corpses and causes funerals while promising his victims a safe passage, good harvest, and numerous children—the blessings of earth to replace those of eternal gain.

I hate this god who stole destinies, who fashioned this world of violent confusion, this deceiver who has hidden our histories, disguised his own misdeeds and cast blame upon his own victims.

And I know I am not alone. Others have the sight, they perceive that this shell is a copy, not a world. The chords of my soul vibrate in resonance to the presence of a rising collective who are going to see and do great things. Waymakers. Torches lit like impenetrable safe havens in a growing darkness.

The song of my spirit longs to leave, to pass on to the Other Side, to begin a new avatar so when the Doomshape reappears I could be young, strong and ready.

But this is fantasy. I know I am meant to pass through the coming fire, to survive and prepare the way for those who are still blinded by this Demiurge, whom my soul despises.

This trickster... his delusions so perfect. His next machination will be his magnum opus, his Sistine Chapel... "to deceive if it were possible even the very elect."

You are the Sojourner

It was under a violent sky that you first came to the surface. From the Deep you emerged with others who sought to explore the World Above. It was not long before you laid eyes upon The Others... those people who had survived from The World Before... who had forgotten everything as they had remained on the surface.

The centuries passed and you found yourself at a potter's wheel for a vintner of Badtibira of the Pentopolis, before it was buried in Typhon Flood. You sailed on in spirit to emerge in the Land Between the Rivers.

In the dust of ancient Sumer, where the Tigris and Euphrates whispered secrets, you were born. A farmer, toiling under the relentless sun, planting seeds that echoed your own cycle of rebirth. Your hands, weathered and wise, sowed the first chapter of an epic journey.

As the pages of time turned, you emerged in Assyria, an artisan sculpting stories in stone. With each chisel stroke, you captured the might of kings, only to crumble like your own creations, succumbing to the sands of time.

On Phoenician shores, you, now a daring navigator, harnessed the winds, your sails blooming like the purple dye that colored your city's fame. In the embrace of the sea, you found your demise, leaving whispers in the waves.

In the heart of Egypt, beneath the shadow of pyramids, you lived as a scribe. Hieroglyphs danced from your fingers, a ballet of ink and papyrus. But even you, a chronicler of eternity, fell prey to a plague, your stories outliving your breath.

In Persia's grandeur, you, adorned in silk, whispered counsel in the ears of kings. A vizier, wise yet unseen, until the blade of intrigue cut your thread of life.

Amidst the glory of Greece, you, a philosopher, pondered the mysteries of existence. Yet, in irony's embrace, found your end in hemlock's bitter kiss.

In the Roman Empire, you marched, a legionnaire, shield and sword in hand. In battle's fiery dance, you fell, leaving your valor as a testament to time.

In Constantinople, you, a spirited merchant, traded goods and tales alike. Yet fate, the greatest merchant of all, bartered your life for a plague's cruel touch.

In Merovingian France, your voice rang out in court, a minstrel weaving tales of love and loss. But even your melodies could not deter the silent approach of age.

In the shadows of Wallachia, you, a monk, transcribed ancient texts, your ink a bridge between worlds. Yet, in the irony of fate, you perished in a fire, your own words fueling the flames.

As a Viking, you roared across seas, a warrior fierce and unyielding. Yet, in the irony of a peaceful shore, you met your end, not in battle, but in the quiet embrace of sickness.

In Norman times, you built castles, stone by stone, a mason with dreams as lofty as his towers. But dreams are fragile, and you fell from the very heights you sought to conquer.

In Anglo-Saxon lands, you, a farmer once again, plowed the earth, history repeating in furrows and fields. But war knows no boundaries, and you fell to a conqueror's sword.

In Ireland, you whispered with the wind, a Druid, keeper of ancient lore. Yet, even you, attuned to nature's rhythm, could not escape the march of time, succumbing to the quiet end of a life well-lived.

In the misty hills of Wales, you became a bard, your voice carrying the weight of legends and songs.

In your melodies, the Druidic echoes of past lives resonated, until your voice faded with the setting sun.

In the bustling streets of Victorian England, you, now a watchmaker, crafted timepieces, each tick a reminder of your own temporal journey. Yet, in a twist of fate, you were claimed by the very time you sought to measure.

On the turbulent seas, you hoisted sails as a pirate under the East India Company's shadow. In the pursuit of treasure and freedom, you found your end, not by sword or storm, but by betrayal's sharp sting.

In North American colonies, you, a fervent patriot, fought for a new beginning. Your ideals, as bullet and blade, clashed in revolution's fiery heart, where you fell, your dreams birthing a nation.

Finally, in modern Germany, you walk as a scholar, a fusion of past wisdom and present knowledge. In libraries and streets, you seek the threads of your past lives, each step a journey through history's tapestry.

Each life, a verse in an eternal poem, each death, a pause before the next stanza. For eight minutes, this narrative unfolds, a symphony of lives lived and lost, echoing the eternal dance of you through the corridors of time.

You are the immortal within... these experiences are life-sims in the field of the Oversoul. Each unfolding act in the spiritual drama is a ripening of the harvest soon to come. Each death is a chrysalis shed from a growing soul on its way to being adopted into an Infinity unknown until experienced. You are the king and serf, the learned and ignorant, the carefree and oppressed. We have all been helmsmen at the fore, or rowers expending our strength just to ensure another's passage and at times, some of us have even walked the plank. We are both the poem and poet and in these dark times we are both the observer and the standard-bearer that are both unmoved in this war for the soul, because the Fight was never ours.

You're in a Divine Video Game—Deal With It

Modern science has revealed that information is a fundamental building block of the universe, and that the universe behaves like a massive computer. This could be seen as evidence that the universe is a simulation created by an advanced civilization. Quantum physics suggests that reality is dependent on the observer and that particles can exist in multiple states simultaneously. By applying this understanding we can imagine that the universe is a digital construct, and reality is only "rendered" when it is observed.

The philosopher Nick Bostrom's argument proposes that it's more likely that we are living in a simulation created by a more advanced civilization, based on the idea that technological civilizations will eventually be able to simulate entire universes. And perhaps on a deeper level we agree, for the idea that we are living in a simulation has become a popular theme in science fiction, movies, and video games. This could be seen as evidence that the idea of a simulated reality is resonating with people on a subconscious level.

But this Game has an Overseer that will expend much energy in preventing this discovery. Let us be clear—if this reality is a simulation (and much evidence points to this fact), then it is far more advanced than anything we can imagine. I originally attempted a detailed overview of it from our current "gaming" perspective, but it comes nowhere near the immense power and sophistication that we are up against. Whatever oversees the simulation has not only entrapped us and kept us blind to its machinations, but controls the entire natural world, all of its interlocking parts, and somehow controls all of the most important outcomes reached in order to maintain its control.

The player in the Game has subjected himself to its dictates... but there is still hope. There is an exception. The immortal errant goes another way because he at least understands, to a point, the predicament. Errants and a few others possess the secret knowledge of how this system works. They cannot hide, because energy is perceived by the Overseer. And to the awakened immortals, the Overseer will open the gates of Hades and cast forth its minions. Not to quell what cannot be killed, but to isolate and sequester, so this immortal-ness will not awaken others whose lamps have yet been lit.

We can choose directions, select missions and achievements, can manage possessions and apparel—all within the simulation. Even death is simulated. The Player "respawns" each morning after a brief time out, which is often hidden in the phenomenon of sleep and then waking up to a new day. We are alive not because we haven't died— we are alive because we *cannot* die.

The blind masses play deeper into the labyrinths and the immortal errants who play the field, seeing the board for what it is, reap the pleasure of its mastery. They come to comprehend the armor of God, and the minions of AIX —Artificial Intelligence X—fall as pieces across the board.

In such a controlled environment, choice is illusory but the rich detail of the construct and the variables offered as a panoramic field to the Player become so convincing that the Player easily gets absorbed into the narratives the construct builds.

The immortal errant goes by unexpected ways, passes through the construct by paths unseen by others, while the Overseer watches, schemes, anticipates and moves the pieces across the board to checkmate the Player before his light heals yet another blind pawn.

As we develop more sophisticated virtual reality systems and approximations of artificial intelligence, it is becoming apparent, more and more each day, that we are living in one ourselves.

Our senses can only perceive a limited range of frequencies and wavelengths, and there are many things that exist beyond our perception. This could be interpreted as evidence that the universe is a digital construct, and our perception is limited by the simulation.

In around 1950, famed physicist Enrico Fermi came up with what has since been known as the Fermi paradox. It presents us with the quandary of there being such a high probability for an advanced form of intelligent, extraterrestrial life along with the fact that there is no evidence for it whatsoever, with us staring out into an unfathomably huge and empty universe.

There is no paradox in Fermi because there are no alien races hiding in the holography. Pathetic Players shake their heads in agreement at pawns who cling to hopes in Galactic Federations and Pleiadeans that live not in space, but in fertile minds.

What we've learned about our reality reveals an ever-lurking suspicion that we are not really here, or that we do not belong... we are longing for a home we can't seem to find. We know that it is not here.

In our search from within this earthly dungeon realm, there is a voice that stills our souls. It beckons us to *look*, to pay attention. Events can sometimes become changed, commonalities within familiar memories are erased and altered so that what has been etched in memory is now phantasmically changed. The Mandela Effect occurs when large groups of people share in the same false memory of an event. In this we have a friend that beckons us to know that the construct can be changed, and little changes infer that the All can be altered.

The immortal laughs at these glitches, deeming deja'vu and silly synchronicities as evidence of the Overseer's inability to totally control the Board... AIX's inherent limitations and imperfections.

We move through the maelstrom applying the finesse of a zombie etiquette that frees us to move impetuously through the maze.

In the context of a simulated world the Overseer of the holofield would be able to anticipate a Player's moves to a great degree because the terrain modifies the choices, and NPCs are thrown in to deter, guide and distract. In standard gaming, an NPC is a non-player character—a mindless character unable to think for itself, only there to follow a pre-determined script.

In a data-filled environment of moving imagery, the Overseer is able to make adjustments, changes, and edits that the Player would almost have no way of perceiving until the edited holography was passed through. Only in retrospect can most of these edits be noticed. But even when a Player of acute sensitivity manages to realize that his holography has been manipulated, the Overseer employs newer scenarios, problems and NPCs to distract from any deep contemplation.

The key of the Overseer protocols is to keep the Player in a reactive mode, responding to situational stimuli, to NPC activity, to the labyrinthine meanderings of decisions to either go right, left, up, down, or back—and to convince this Player that these are the only choices. For the Player, the only reward under these circumstances is survival and the ability to risk one's life yet again under different circumstances.

The Overseer has the advantage of a database that stores all the knowledge of the Player Archives, an immense collection of the cause-and-effect records of past Player activity that informs the Overseer of the choices one would likely make under specific circumstances. This is why reality seems to anticipate what individuals do, why our environments seem to respond to our choices. The presence of patterns, coincidences, synchronicity, Mandelbrot geometry, and fractals in our experience can be seen as evidence that our experience is being generated by a complex, mathematical simulation.

If you don't know the players you're not even in the Game. NPCs haunt the programming and fill the terrain with distraction and dungeon programming. The Agent Smiths patrol the holography seeking pattern breaks; they are Men in Black sent forth to police the chaos choreographed by an Adjustment Bureau armed by trolls, the status quo, and virus programs issued forth to separate the free from the sea of slaves. They patrol Elysium in their effort to keep the Players in the Game.

The errant is a highly individualized pattern-breaking soul in a system of controlled chaos.

The errant is an anomaly so mysterious to the AI Overseer that it has to manipulate its own programming to deal with them.

The observer-dependent nature of the simulation allows for multiple realities to coexist within the same simulation, each with its own set of perceived evidence to support it. The AI manipulates the perception and observation of individuals within the simulation to create an observer-dependent hologram, where the perceived reality is shaped by the observer's individual experiences and perspectives. While this works to control the Players and slaves, it is the errant who sees through the deceit.

The AI once generated ample evidence to support the idea of a flat world and now generates evidence to support mostly a globular world through manipulation of physical observations, data, and historical records. But the errant isn't fooled by the two choices, knowing that the construct transcends both the plane and the sphere.

Unique theories, inventions, and suddenly appearing concepts and ideas throughout history can manifest through individuals with sensitive minds who absorb this data from the thought-field, which contains data and artifacts from previous simulations. The underlying data structures in a simulation are often designed to exhibit repeating patterns and self-similar structures.

Cartographic manipulation is used to create false narratives or obscure events that the AI deems necessary to keep hidden in order to hide the occurrence of a reset. Coincidences and synchronicity suggest that events or experiences are not happening by chance but are instead following a predetermined pattern or structure.

The errant is of spiritual nonlocality, unpredictable, undefinable and not subject to the dungeon programming embracing the masses. The errant as an immortal observes the chaos beyond the board, but the Player stays a slave, bound to the refuse that is spewed from Pandora's vase.

The Magical Architecture of Reality

One who is properly informed is not easily deceived.

We are more than we suppose ourselves to be. True power in bringing what we want to us requires us to understand that the very medium of simulated holography we exist within is alive, it is aware. It also responds to us only when we perform a single deliberate act, as described below.

First, it is important to remember that we do not escape the dark by ignoring the shadows. The positive thinking theory of law of attraction teachers has done more harm than good. I will instead present to you a simple formula to get what you want in life, and with this new understanding you will better comprehend the mechanics of this world, so that you may or may not believe that it is a simulation.

The vast majority of people live in defaulted, unchanging, unimaginative lives, continuing down a simulated reality tunnel that makes little allowance for change or the introduction of new experiences. The living reality matrix entombs these people in default programming and has no cause for heightened scrutiny of their unchanging lives. The thoughts and dreams of these people flash across the tunneled holography and disappear because they have no power—the thoughts are not followed by activity.

But as soon as a personality moves in an unanticipated direction, breaches the reality tunnel through the related continued activity and creates momentum, the reality matrix does two things immediately. First, it constructs new and better experiences for the rogue spirit, to keep it from returning to the default environment and cause a spread of this behavior. Second, the former negative default reality tunnel, as a means of system control, empowers people still living inside it to regard the free spirt as an anomaly, a rebel to be shunned, a malfunctioning human.

The system we live inside is all about conservation of energy, and the best way to conserve power is to have multitudes chained into dungeon tunnels of reality that hardly ever change. Circuits that operate on the same frequency keep the board easily powered and are predictably controlled.

The free spirit, however, is empowered to create their own life and reality, and when this happens reality reciprocates. It is because this holospheric reality matrix we live within is the construction of a mind that fears a total awakening of the imprisoned spirits. For this reason, the vagabond, free-thinking individual begins to receive all that they desire. The holosphere's campaign kicks in to keep the empowered spirit from awakening so many others, otherwise there will come an inevitable system overload, a shutdown—resulting in the total loss of power by this mind that has imprisoned immortal beings, beings who have been deluded into believing they are powerless humans.

Now, knowing this, and understanding that this belief about who and what we *really* are derives from antiquity, and was a major tenet of the Vedic and later Gnostic teachings, how can you personally use this information to empower yourself, to change the negative circumstances of your life into a life of fun, awe, inspiration, plenty and happiness? In 1919 Ernest Holmes wrote that the average person, when told the truth, will still seek some other way. I hope you, my listener, are not this type of person.

Be honest with yourself. In your life, have you sat back quietly and watched someone who is more outspoken and more physically active and more open to new ideas step out and try to accomplish something, and it seems like nothing they do is wrong, or even when they make a step in the wrong direction it ends up turning out the right way?

One needs to understand the mechanics of our reality and the rules it operates by. Watching and taking notes from a hundred YouTube self-help law of attraction videos will never allow one to comprehend this plastic medium that we are immersed within. The holography that we live in is a reflective medium, like a mirror. When you are not actively heading in a certain direction in your life, when you are not actively trying to build something, when you are not trying to meet someone, when you are not trying to accomplish something, and when you are not trying to learn something, then you are existing in stasis. You now become a victim to other people's reality tunnels, because your own reality tunnel has stagnated.

Said another way, if you quit trying to live the life you want, then you will quickly drown in the lives of others.

Our simulated holography responds to you according to the energy input that you put into your idea. If you are taking yourself seriously, and believe in what you are doing, then reality itself conforms to your wants, it begins bringing into contact those very things that you're trying to do: bringing people, situations, circumstances and physical objects into your life that will help you accomplish what it is you're trying to do. In fact, the more you head in a certain direction, the more crystallized your path becomes, and the holosphere is way ahead of you, like a chess game. This reality matrix is three moves ahead of you at all times.

Make no mistake, we exist within a magical medium, a magical construction so plastic and receptive that it responds not only to our thoughts, but it changes when we make any single action in any direction that has intent behind it. If you treat your everyday reality as an enemy, the world will make war against you, there will be no peace. Your belief will guarantee the perpetuation of your afflictions, because reality will always give you what you perceive to be true.

Just take a moment to free yourself of the default negative programming of our world. One minute, 60 seconds, is all that is required: Just breathe as deeply as you can, and exhale, then breathe and exhale, and you will find your body resonating in a frequency that you rarely experience—breathing is the code. You will become more euphoric, and at this exact time you need to change your mode of thinking. You need to think and be convinced that the universe is your friend. You need to wake up in the morning and thank the universe for being your friend, and you will quickly see evidence of a reciprocal nature. Reality will begin manifesting experiences in your life that will perpetuate the understanding that reality is indeed your friend. The default negative programming that is covering your life and created your pessimism and negativity and sorrow and anguish will melt away, as positive experiences and people come into your life.

Reality will perpetuate the condition that proves as true — whatever it is that your opinion maintains, whether it be that you are friends or enemies with the universe.

This cerebral interface holography that we're immersed within reacts to us, it is both our freedom and prison. It does not matter your education, it does not matter your ability to understand the deeper mysteries of life, these have absolutely no bearing on what's happening to you on a daily basis. Every moment of every day is absolutely pregnant with possibility, but from the time we wake up in the morning we are immediately immersed into this sense perception of illusions that make us believe that "we cannot do this, we should not do that." What we don't think we can accomplish through thoughts like, "I don't believe I can do this, I believe that I can't do this"— these types of thoughts solidify and crystallize the holography around us that keeps us from doing the very things that we fear we cannot do. People who are subject to the default programming of our reality have edited out of their awareness any possibility for miracles, any potentiality beyond what is conceived as the normal human spectrum of experience.

But for those who truly see that they are not a body, but a divine being encased in mortal trappings for a temporary time, they completely edit for themselves a whole new reality. If I am a spirit existing in a world that is simulated to make me believe that I am physical, and I am truly the mode of force of the creative world around me that I experience, and if I am the cause of the simulated holography that I suffer... then what can I do with this information? How do I alter the trajectory of my life forward into the life that I want to live? How do I apply this information, to transform into the powerful person that I know deep inside I was meant to be?

The answer is very simple. You are a piece of individualized divinity, a divine spark. You belong to, are connected with, and are made up of the very holographic medium that you exist within. All of your troubles come from your belief that you are disconnected. A chief trait of the default programming we are immersed within is to keep us from moving in any direction. Originality, however, induces subroutines within the holography, to instantly begin giving us the new reality tunnel that we want, that we are building, that we want to experience. Breaking free from dungeon programming requires you to continue to build your momentum in a new direction, to break free from the default programming. In a short time, the default programming itself will completely be overwritten, as the holosphere knits together future events molded before you experience them. Hours, not days, not months—reality is knitted together into a tapestry whose threads were individually woven by your thoughts and the actions you put behind them.

We are immensely powerful creatures, completely immersed into a negative medium that tries to convey, that tries to convince us every moment of every day, that we are not. The power of positive thinking will provide you with more positive thought, but that alone will do nothing for you. All the thinking in the world will only produce more thinking. If thinking alone ever changed anything, then there would be no need to have hundreds of people releasing law of attraction YouTube videos that millions of people continue to listen to. The very existence of successful law of attraction YouTube channels is because they have chosen a reality tunnel which is a self-fulfilling loop—by teaching people the law of attraction they give them hope, but it only produces the *selling* of hope to others who are desperately seeking the same. The feedback loop never ends, because the YouTube channel becomes more successful, selling even more hope to even more people who are searching for it. In the literary world, this is mirrored precisely by the numerous millionaire authors who became rich not by publishing books of originality, but publishing books that teach others how to make money publishing books. The selling of hope, when presented positively, is always a success only to the seller—ask any honest preacher.

Make a decision about who you want to be and what you want to experience. Decide in your mind and stick to it. And while you're thinking about what you want to do or who you want to be, you must move forward and never retreat. The default programming of negativity will respond instantly if you're heading in the right direction, it will try to stop you from leaving your reality tunnel. When it collapses, you will never go back to it again. Oliver Wendell Holmes said it best. "When the human mind is stretched by a new idea, it can never go back to its original dimensions."

Actions with intent is activity that induces our environment to respond to it.

When we are inactive, our environment afflicts us with the sensations that perpetuate within us the sensations that we are physical beings, stuck at a certain location at a certain time.

But when it is we who are moving, when we are paying attention, when it is we who are active in a certain direction, then it is our environment that is responding to us.

When we are in motion, other people's reality tunnels do not afflict us. When we are in motion, we are practicing our divinity, our divine ability as creators of the world we live in. But when we are still and doing nothing, we are absolutely subject to the worlds that are built by others.

So make a decision. Decide and imagine the experiences that you want. And when you've given this sufficient thought, and you have decided that you are ready to change your world, then you make a decision and you do something *different*—you go somewhere else, engage in activity that you have never done before, knowing that originality *always* possesses powers of its own.

If you're going to tap into the absolutely unfathomable and immeasurable resources of the universe, to create and build, then you need to step out of the reality tunnel that you've chained yourself to.

Once this intelligent holospheric medium realizes that you are serious, that you have made an executive decision, governing the parameters of your life, that you have acted on it, then you will instantly see the very architecture of your existence changing before you, with brand new emotions, new people, new circumstances, new things coming into your life with ease.

Thought that you back up with action is immediately taken up into the magical construction as a blueprint, and it will begin building for you the instant that you provide momentum.

If you want to change your world, you need to change what you are doing. A simple conscious decision not to continue a certain life pattern or a single activity that goes against what you have been previously doing, instantly opens up an entirely new reality tunnel in this simulated holography.

We open up parallel universes every single day, when we take a new direction from where we were going in the previous moment.

Make a decision. Imagine what you want, then act on it. I assure you, the universe has a vested interest in making sure you get what you want—it's not a benign interest.

Chapter Seven

EMPOWER THE IMMORTAL

There is a Wizard Within You

There is a power in boldness, assertiveness. There is a fundamental power in confidence—it cannot be measured, it's not quantifiable. Reality itself is nonlocal, the human imagination is not governed by anything that's measurable in Newtonian physics.

Our lives are magical. The negativity, the pain we suffer is because we come into contact with other people's reality tunnels, which happen because information from these worlds we came into contact with was accepted as true. There is no blame; we are programmed to accept things we come into contact with. Yes, the default programming of our existence is negative in the collective, but in the personal we have great power to create great things in our lives.

Our holospheric medium is stimulated into activity by the beliefs of those confined within it, a morphic field that continually generates the real out of the imagined. The architecture of reality is so plastic and receptive that it will always produce effects in proportion to the waveforms of our cerebral transmitters. This secret is so simple—act as if you are, and you will be.

I have made a long study of the events of my life and the world around me, allowing me to make these inescapable conclusions: My experiences conform to my picture of reality, my beliefs. The outcome of my endeavors correlate with my expectation. Therefore, my assumptions of truth become the truth. Manifesting what I believe is the function of the universe. The world has no power over me; it merely reflects what I choose to see, confirming my beliefs about myself, which obey no laws, nor are they confined by them.

At all times I am casting out a magnetic image of what I think of myself, attracting to me experiences that correspond with that image. My self-perception creates circumstances that confirm my image of myself. The world responds to me in the precise proportion of how I perceive myself.

Because we live in a fiction, products of our imagination, also fictions, create our reality. My perceptions of natural phenomena and laws of physics are creations of our collective minds that I have accepted as true. But I am not bound by them, for I exist mentally in a dimension beyond the material; therefore, I conjure events into existence by my desire to experience them. I encourage events to move in a certain direction. I alter one reality to create another, to make things happen that would ordinarily not occur. I draw people, events and conditions from absolutely unexpected sources. I originate new conditions out of nothing. I set things in motion that do not diminish over time. I live out the fiction, to create the fact. I change the physical world through practiced intention.

Because 100% of the future is constructed of a union of the real and the imagined, I dream my life into existence, free to create any reality I prefer. Therefore, my creativity possesses powers of its own. My thoughts collapse possibilities into realities. Morphing from one self to another, switching reality tunnels, I instantly induce reality to change—with each self, I assume I bring about an alternate universe.

Existing in a state of non-union, I exercise power over my environment. Independent of existence, I am able to employ any magical technology I will—my own entirely subjective, complete and closed system; it doesn't have to work for anybody else. My own self-created subjective reality is a by-product of my imagination, both entertaining and profiting me.

I deliberately act beforehand to create virtual influences, imaginings that then modify reality. Everything to me is possible and real, because it is all moored to an illusion—this holosphere.

I am moored to a living, etheric field, not the perceived reality tunnels. Because I am a spark amidst an infinite sea of possibility, my experiences are due to the reality tunnels I choose to view the world through. I create experiences by inventing new reality tunnels. I imagine the things I desire, to build informed fields that imprint the ether, drawing them into my physical existence.

Due to these realizations, I conclude with this summary: Products of my imagination are not limited by precedent. In the ether, everything I want already exists. Knowing there is no opposition, opposition cannot appear. Nothing hinders me but myself. My thoughts of power produce power. By acts of imagination, I draw from myself more than I contain. My faith is not conceived and known; it is lived and enacted. By acting as though I am, I become. By my attitude I influence all outcomes.

When I change my attitude, I change my world.

What my mind most contemplates, that I become.

I receive not what I want, but what I am.

Because I am what I am, I become what I will.

Co-Creator Relationship

We live inside an anti-realm, where base matter is convincing, and the spirit is confined—it is the photonegative of a real reality that is somewhere else.

Inside this construct, the truth is always perpetuated through fictions. It is the realm of the liar, where the exact opposite of the truth must be uttered in order to make it true.

But in this dungeon of the demiurge, the Oversoul has provided a way to use the rules of this construct to reach the individualized souls trapped inside. In this construct, the soul is encouraged to speak those things that be not as if they are, and act as if it is so, so it will be. And to those lost in this darkness, this secret is absolute foolishness—those souls that are lost focus on what is, as opposed to what can be.

You see, a problem must never be made the focus of awareness. As a co-creator, you must do the exact opposite. You must act as if the solution already exists, and your physical avatar must act as if what is wanted is already possessed.

My books and videos are the result of me believing that that knowledge is not lost; it just hasn't been found yet. That the truth is not unknown; it just hasn't been told yet.

When I delve into my researches, I do so with the belief that there is no end to the discoveries I can find, and that in each session I concentrate on my notes and my books, I know that in the end the result will be a presentation that others will find value in. By adopting this mindset, that the end result is already secure, then the methods I employ to find these things are no longer guided by me, which has limitations, but guided by intuition and imagination. And these are empowered by the Oversoul.

When we adopt this idea as a guiding principle, that the end is secure, then we can know for certain that all steps leading up to this final result are secure as well.

The thought that great effort is required to accomplish a desired end only ensures that great effort will be required. The informed field of the individual broadcasts the conditions expected into the neutral field of the construct—the Simulacrum—and this field begins to move all the pieces that are already in the field into position to fulfill the upload.

If you hold that certain conditions must be met before fulfillment, then what you want will be kept away from you until those conditions are met. You must imagine the end result as if it is already a set of conditions that exists.

The idea that you are the cause, the builder of your future, will hinder your efforts. The idea that God will give you what you want hasn't worked for hundreds of millions of people who are still praying for change. Remember, the prayer of desperation admits a situation for what it is, and thus continues it. Both positions deny a key fundamental, which has everything to do with how the Oversoul sees us as individuals.

To be a co-creator means this is a shared experience. This implies that who we share it with seeks to know that we are fully engaged in a relationship with it.

The dynamic is simple: The individualized soul projects a set of conditions and experiences it wants to bring into personal reality, and the Oversoul, through the neutral field of the Simulacrum, only brings to pass those conditions in accordance with the measure of energy broadcast into it, because it is restricted in its ability by the very parameters of this relationship, between itself and the individual soul. And the parameters of this relationship are completely dictated by the amount of trust the soul has in the Oversoul. This is what true faith is—it is trust that the soul knows it is worthy, and trust is absolutely required in any relationship.

Looked at inversely, the Oversoul will build for you the world you want, the more you trust its willingness and ability to do so. Your ability to dictate your world and future is 100% dependent on your relationship with the Oversoul, and this relationship is 100% dependent upon you.

During the first part of your life you are growing, learning, adapting to the world, living in a reactive mindset, and therefore all the way into your 20s and 30s you are merely living in the reality tunnels built by others.

In your 30s and 40s you are now responsible for the conditions of your world, your reality, and many of these conditions came through living other people's realities, accepting the world through the lens of others' beliefs.

But now you're actively creating your world and contributing to the construct, which provides worlds for others. It is at this time the more advanced souls wake up to this relationship and begin building fantastic lives. Most only awaken in their 50s and 60s, but the transformation in their lives is real, genuine, and completely the result of this relationship status between the Oversoul and the individual who has begun to awaken, after a lifetime of experiences that have shown the patterns of mistakes and victories.

In your mind, take a picture of the future, a snapshot of you with all the conditions you want to experience. Thank the Oversoul for receiving this picture from you. Feel gratitude that this is now who you are and what you experience.

Your activity in life must infer that you already possess that which you projected. This patterning sends strong signals into the neutral field, that a thing already exists, therefore the Simulacrum brings it into existence. It's that simple.

Co-Creators Weave Fiction into Facts

I fully understand that I am an informed field, I am a soul, a spirit, an immortal being trapped in this false holography. This world is the exact opposite of almost everything it should be. Think about it. This predator-versus-prey ecosphere, where the wolf can rend the rabbit to gain its sustenance... Where is the morality in that? And I understand that there are many defenders of natural selection, the uniformitarian theory, and they believe that good and evil should never be attributed to the animal kingdom, I get that. But I do know that mother birds nurture their young; lion mothers, they also nurture their young. And yes, I understand you can fall back on pure science and say, "Well, that's just visceral, that's all instinctual," and I get that. But there is nothing holy about a great white shark and what it can do to the human body, nothing.

This world, it's not what we think it is—it's something else. And when great evil and violence is promoted and propagated, and even those who perpetuate those activities are even rewarded, then the world is not what we think it is, or at least it's not what we've been taught to believe it is.

Projecting the present is what most of the world does, that's what they do, and this is why they never break out of their paradigm. This is why they're still worried about the future, 30 years after they have graduated high school, they're still worried about all these exact same things they were worried about when they first graduated from high school and knew they had to enter the job market and make a living, and they had to do all that! Yet, you're *still* worried about paying the bills, you're still worried about social standing, you're still worried if you're in the right religion, you're still worried about a whole lot of external things that are nothing but the dressings on a dungeon, that's all they are—you are still projecting the present.

Projecting the present is what we're trained to do since we were little kids. And what I mean by projecting is that we are essentially building thought forms, and releasing them multiple times a day through expectation, through anxiety, through daydreaming.... We imagine what we're going to do tomorrow, and the next day, and we're actually building our reality. Those anxieties, they form an imprint into the neutral field of the holosphere. We're building our own problems over and over.

Projecting the present is equally as bad as projecting the past—which is another class of people. Most people project the present, but there's another group that is focused more on the past. This aspect of dungeon programming has them isolating particulars in the distant past that, in their own minds, they feel have meaning, so they somehow become chained to incidents in the past that prevent them from moving forward into a better future.

Projecting the past is basically an admission that the past is a predicate for the future, or at least your future. To avoid any confusion about projecting the present and projecting the past, one should understand that I'm only talking about it on the personal level. Many people new to my work do not understand the intricacy of this construct; others more familiar have gained this understanding through the large amount of freely given material that describes how it works.

In general, you are existing within two separate independent realities as you are listening to my voice. One reality is the personal, it is the one that you know, it is the highly individualized immortal soul listening to my voice right now; the other reality that you're existing in is an Oversoul construct, it is a confluence of programming templates of all kinds of reality tunnels that we, as a collective, are travelling through. It's using all kinds of backdrop programming, it's dungeon programming, negative default programming.

Within all this we are experiencing, as a group, a world that is saturated with media programming, and it's saturated with cultural and racial and intellectual programming, and we basically pick and choose how we navigate through this morass, this maelstrom of programming that is designed to impede the immortal being from moving forward.

There are two separate realities. One of them is the highly individual you, it is the immortal spark, it is the soul which has an informed field. That informed field possesses every iota of data you have ever absorbed in your entire life, now and in all the life-sims that you have been travelling in while in this construct. However many lifetimes you've lived before, you have acquired data, your informed field builds up. This informed field is what nature responds to, it's also what gives you power over your environment, and over the minds of others you come in contact with. It makes them pay attention to you.

On the surface people don't know your depth, but intrinsically their own informed fields are neutralized by the presence of a powerful informed field who has awakened and who knows who he or she is. There are those who understand that they are immortal, and that the construct no longer has power over them, and if this is the case with you, it may be close to being your last time going through this dungeon realm. Because once the construct realizes that it has been perceived as such, then you're now a threat. You might not be coming back in to experience another life-sim; you're going to be ejected, you're going to be sent off into the next construct, or back home, or wherever that is.

In this reality we are dealing with the here and now, and in the here and now the vast majority of souls trapped in this construct are projecting the present, therefore tomorrow is still operating off the present, therefore the day after tomorrow is still their present, and, for example, 3522 days into future they are still living the exact lifestyle they were living 3522 days earlier. They have projected the present, and as a co-creator this, and only this, was honored—their informed field built their future, and then they lived it—there is no one to blame but themselves.

Projecting the past is equally bad. Because these souls have been traumatized into believing that something in their past has chained them and they are unable to move forward—it's equally bad. They believe that the past is a predicate for the future for the individual, a belief that locks them in place.

The past is not a predicate for the individual. Remember, you're in two separate realities, and they are governed by different rules. You are the law in the personal, but not in the construct. And this is a hard pill to swallow; many of you have come to my YouTube channel thinking that you're going to find the recipe for how to save the world, and you've found just the opposite. I have told you in presentation after presentation that we are not here to save the world, because the world is an artificial construct, and everything here is just the opposite of what it should be.

We're living in the photonegative of a real reality, even our arithmetic hints to a greater arithmetic beyond and I've shown you the mathematical experiments. We are living in nil space, we're living in something that is absolutely artificial. There's no better way than to say it is a Simulacrum, which is a copy of something that is real somewhere else.

So, this world thrives on deception, on lies, on violence—these are the hallmarks of its creator. Remember, even in the New Testament we are told that Satan is the god of this world. He's not God, and he's not the God of the universe; he's the god of this world. This is the same as the Gnostic viewpoint, where the Demiurge is the creator of this false construct that immortal souls are passing through. I'm in agreement with both of those tenets.

Though I am not a Christian, I agree that something negative created this construct, but something positive on the outside of the construct has basically allowed for the very deceit of the construct itself to be our greatest ally—this is another hard pill to swallow. Remember, Jesus did not speak the truth; he spoke in parables, parables are images of truth, they're not the truth—those stories didn't happen, therefore they are fictions.

So, one should not project the present, and we should not project the past. They are traps, as just explained in detail. The true immortal, the awakened individual, the highly individualized immortal soul inside the construct, the co-creators among the race... We are they who project temporary falsehoods to create positive facts. We imagine what isn't, but pretend that it is, and it comes to pass. This is the method we use. It's not the law of attraction; it's the law of reflection. This is because we are in a construct that operates like a spiritual hologram, a reflective mirror-like hologram that responds to the etheric temerity of spirit. It works this way because empathy, intuition and imagination are purely spiritual. Therefore, using those three positive powers together, we build pictures in our mind of what tomorrow is going to be like, and then we follow through, we project this, and then we act as if we are, so we will be.

We pretend that something that we know as false is actually true, and therefore it becomes real to us. I tell you all the time—our world is not what you think!

This should be a soul-empowering message, but for some of you it may be a stumbling block. You may not be ready or willing to try, and that's okay. But I'm telling you now—we are immortal beings trapped in a deceitful, mirror-like holographic field, and it reflects as circumstances the very things we project into it. And it's a neutral field. It does not care about fact or fiction, it does not care about true or false, it does not care about good or evil. These are things that you, as an immortal being, must work out with the Oversoul. Inside the construct, there are no barriers to the creative process if one knows how to proceed.

If you want to be a co-creator, if you want to receive the inheritance that was already given you, then don't project the present, or all you will get is the present. It's not that you're neutralizing the creative process; it's that you're using it to create a repetitive program, you are using your creative power to create a duplicate of today onto the template of tomorrow—it's entirely your fault, you can blame no one else.

Equally, those of you who disregard the present as inconsequential, but hold onto intangibles from the past... You're holding on to events, you're holding on to experiences in your past that you believe are stopping you from becoming who you want to be tomorrow. This is the victim mentality, and it is very popular in psychology; they actually promote it.

But it's your fault for not moving forward, because the chains that are connected to your past are entirely created by you *imagining* that they exist.

So, you can equally break them, break free or die trying, this is what the construct is about. It's about the immortal soul not only learning who he or she is, but learning that they're a co-creator, and that every experience that they have, moving forward, is entirely of their own making. I'm not talking about little kids who get victimized, I'm not talking about grown people who have not developed.

There's a certain stage in the period of human development where the soul and the psyche finally unite, morals are fixed and people understand—it's called maturity, and there's a reason for that. There are a lot of people who die and exit the construct before they're ever given a chance to experience maturity; they're still adolescent when they're victimized in some way or murdered or when they suffer an accident. For whatever reasons, the Oversoul thought it fit that that soul should be removed from the construct at that time. We don't know what the Oversoul had planned, we don't know these things, so we can't beat up ourselves over these issues.

What we can know is our personal self. And if you want to project the present, then by all means do so, but don't complain tomorrow when your tomorrow is an exact duplicate of the boring-ass life you have today. If that happens it's because you are using your creative capacity to endorse that, and it's your fault. It's the same for those of you who are chained to the past.

But for the true creator... We speak things that are not as they are. We do the same thing Jesus did: we project "falsehoods." This construct was built by the arch-deceiver. This construct, this predator versus-prey ecosphere, this dungeon programming that accelerates evil and gives power to the most violent, including mass murderers, warped genocidal leaders, the war dogs... These are the ones that are at the top, they're at the top. Why? Because this construct *rewards* them, because they have recognized that it's not about morality, it's not about good or evil, it's not about true or false.

We are what we repeatedly do, and if you don't ever change your itinerary, then no new reality tunnels can ever be built for you. And it's entirely your fault.

Don't project the present, and do not project the past. You must project a falsehood.

If you're not happy today, if you don't have the things you want in life today, but you imagine that you have them, and you look into the future projecting that, and you imagine a better future, and you imagine that three weeks from now you'll have a much better vehicle, you'll have much better living conditions, and you'll be surrounded by people that are more like you, that can strengthen and edify you, that can build you up, but you don't have that now, then there's nothing wrong with that. Yes, it's a falsehood but there's nothing wrong with that. Because if you truly believe that your circumstances can change quickly, and that they're going to change for the better, it can. There's power in that. You don't even have to attach any particulars to it; you can just feel it. Because empathy is spiritual.

One does not just empathize with other people, no—it's a spiritual phenomenon that you can use for yourself. You can feel the feelings of an alternate you living in an alternate timeline, with a whole alternate reality so divorced from anything you are presently experiencing, and when you start moving in that direction to make it happen, you can let the Oversoul do the rest. Because you have projected a falsehood, it's not true in the present, which is dungeon programming. But the freedom lies in that you *imagined* it as something very soon to occur, and you feel that that is the truth, therefore this reflective medium is going to reflect back as circumstances what the individual spirit projected as true, because an actual reflection cannot be distorted—it's not going to make you into a liar.

There's going to be a commiseration. As you move forward in your daily life, excited about how your daily life is changing, your daily life will change. This will endorse the excitement, which will create a feedback loop where you will imagine more particulars about this wonderful new life you have, which will make you more excited. This energy field emanating from your informed field will be absorbed by the neutral field as *factual*, it's like a steady stream of data. You are sending programming into the neutral field of the construct itself, and the construct—which is a neutral field, and doesn't care either way—will receive those instructions and begin knitting for you the very picture you had formed in your mind, because the amplitude, this emotion behind it, is accelerating the process. And the more you see the signs in your daily life of these individual changes getting closer to that period that you envisioned, the more the feedback loop is enforced, the more it grows. Because the more you see the changes, the more excited you get, the more excited you get the neutral field reads that as factual, because you're experiencing it. Therefore, if you are excited about certain conditions, and the neutral field hasn't yet brought those conditions into your existence, then it will speed up the process and bring those conditions into your existence.

You cannot project the present, because then you're programming the Simulacrum to do what it does best—to be a neutral field, in static mode, just shoving the entire human collective through a series of protocols, with you along for the ride. You cannot project the past, because then you're basically programming the construct to create barriers for you that will never let you move forward. It traps you because you have imagined and painted with emotion the power of these chains connecting you to the past, therefore you're fixed and you can't go forward, and the neutral field won't let you. It will never bring new experiences into your existence because you have written the program based on the past and it's going to make you live it.

You have got to project falsehood. You, the highly individualized soul, is forced to be a deceiver in order to create a truth. That is the key, so process that for a minute.

Tell me this world is not evil. The arch-deceiver, who is a murderer from the beginning of human records, has created a false reality that has imprisoned immortal beings. And in order for the immortal beings to get the things that they want in the construct, they too must participate in the lies. Project a falsehood.

This construct is not holy at all—it's simply a neutral field. It will receive any programming and reflect it back as circumstances. The stronger the programming, the better the circumstances. The main rule to remember is that the construct was created with deceit, and it is only operative by deceit.

Think about mass media: what does mainstream media do? They tell us lies all the time! But many lies of ten years ago have become today's truths! It happens all the time—it's a poison, absolute poison. That's how dungeon programming is enforced.

You need to understand how powerful you are. You are already in a position to program the informed field. The informed field that carries all this information, it does not have to cerebrally be present; it's already there. Animals perceive your aura, nature perceives your aura, your aura can be read by the trees that you lean against, and they respond. This informed field is the programming field that allows you to interface with your environment and make whatever changes you want to make.

There are no barriers in life, so I move forward. I envision that I'm going to meet the people I need to meet, I envision that I'm going to come in contact with the data that I need to come in contact with, I envision that I will talk to the people across YouTube and podcasts that I need to talk to. I envision all these things. I let nothing stand before me, nothing.

We cannot remain chained to the past. That's victim mentality, and victim programming produces the victim of tomorrow. I'm not going be that. I'm going move forward, because that's exactly what we're supposed to be doing.

This reality is a construct, and it requires us to be deceitful in order to perform this amazing spiritual alchemy that we're performing. The lies become the truth. And it shouldn't be this way, but this is how it is inside the construct.

And this is how the elite govern us, and how they govern the collective. They already know, they have the receipts—the world they've built is because they've been applying these principles. They know. And some of the most powerful ways to create things are through deceits and deceptions, and in the form of rituals. They do this all the time, right in front of us. They even make us participants by displaying the rituals on television and in the movies; they do it right in front of us, and then the fictions become facts. We turn around and call it predictive programming, when a desired "reality" is projected onto the masses (often meant to control us in some way), and we blindly reinforce it. It was our collective creative capacity the elite used to build the very fiction that they wanted to be turned into a fact. They do it all the time, they use us over and over.

This is a reflective hologram, and it generates experiences out of the imaginings acted upon. Act as if you are, and you will be. There's three main types of souls trapped in this construct.

[1] Those who build their tomorrows to mirror their todays, and they're trapped in dungeon programming.

[2] Those who think tomorrow will never be any different than today because of events in the past. And then there's a small minority, I'm hoping it's you.

[3] A small minority understands that the past is not a predicate for the future, for the highly individualized soul. This small minority understands that all they have to do is imagine something, feel what it is, feel the emotions of having it, and then physically move in that direction. You don't have to follow through, because that's not what a co-creator is all about.

Co-creation is having trust in the construct, in the Oversoul, to fulfill what you started. Because if you think that you have to end or complete something, then you have eliminated the whole co-creator relationship. If you feel that you have to finalize something, then you have essentially told the Oversoul that It's not needed, that you've got this—and that's not a relationship.

The co-creator relationship is that the immortal imagines it, and the construct builds it. It's that simple.

Method of the Co-Creator

Once you realize that an entire lifetime of guilt can be negated with a single act, once you realize that this is the type of Oversoul that we have, that you can be a no good, lousy, sorry SOB your entire life, but when you spiritually hit that wall, and you awaken and realize what you've done, where you are, and what your potential is, and you realize that nothing in the past can stop you from this day forward from doing what you want to do and being who you want to be... once that finally settles in, you will understand the relationship with the Simulacrum. It's a neutral field and, from its perspective, every single moment is pregnant with possibility.

But many individualized souls restrict themselves from moving forward, because they're attached to these chains of the past that we call guilt. When you completely sever those chains, there's nothing to stop you from moving forward, it doesn't matter what your past is. You move forward, accept that relationship with the Oversoul, and when judgement day comes, that's when the details will be ironed out.

But while you're in here, you're subject to a relationship with a neutral field, which is an extension of the Oversoul. The Oversoul is not the creator of this construct. It has made promises to us—that we can do things, we can experience things, we can have things, we can do all this. We can affect other people, we can build spiritual relationships and material relationships, we can do all these things. Because we were granted the position of co-creator, which means that we have to do our part, it also means that the Oversoul will do everything else that we can't do. That's the relationship and it requires trust. You're not going to have that trust if you're still chained to a past.

We can't always invoke the exact particulars we want, and it's not good to try. It shows a lack of trust in the Oversoul when we try to inject detailed, specific answers for whatever the problem is. What we need to do is envision a future that doesn't have these problems, and let the Oversoul—which is very creative, far more creative than we are— to actually bring into our lives all the necessary additives and changes that would smooth that out to where it's much more tolerable. The problem many people have is they cannot move forward because they have attached their psyche to the individual particulars of a problem, and not the solution.

When one envisions a solution, all the particulars of a problem will fade away, they will be solved. This is what the relationship is about. When not capable, one needs to admit that, "I'm not capable of figuring out how I'm going to move forward. This is driving me crazy, I'm at the point of meltdown." One has to admit that their not capable of doing this, and then envision a future where all of this is rectified.

I understand it's difficult, but it can be done. One doesn't have to imagine how things come to pass; that's the business of the Oversoul —this is what It is for.

One has to ascertain what kind of future is wanted, and the Oversoul is going to build that for you, It is going to reciprocate. And whatever these problems are that are important to you right now, they may fade away with solutions that are genius. Things may change in your life so dramatically and so fast that you will look back eight months from now and think, "Damn, I cannot believe how perfect all this unfolded!" and your life is different now, and you have free time and many of the things that you needed.

Like I said, it's not the particulars of anyone's questions or problems that's important. Because we have to look at the fiction. The fiction is, "Everything is okay. Everything is fine. I'm doing good. It's now eight months in the future. I can look back and see how fast everything changed for me, and it's hard to even remember that time when I was listening to that baldheaded dude on YouTube tell me what I needed to do, and I did it... Man, I can't even remember what channel that was now, man, but he changed my life!" Yeah. You'll be very, very surprised how fast things can change for you, but you've got to admit that you're incapable of doing it, you've got to admit that you need help, but you need to move forward despite that. It's a relationship, and you can't think about how things will change; all you have to do is basically project that the change is necessary, and that you're tired, you're done. Giving up is the greatest way to induce change in your life. People holding on to all these different things about the past is the greatest impediment to moving forward.

We know that we are in a false reality. We know this construct still abides by predicates and laws and dictates and subroutines and programs, and it's governed. It's not chaos here—everything is in proportion! We know all about Phi and Pi and 5.108 and curvature equations. We understand entropy, we understand the law of diminishing returns, we understand all these different laws. Listen, this is not a place of chaos; it's only perceived to be by those who don't understand what's transpiring. If everything is the opposite of what it should be here, then you need to create the real you, with the real conditions you want to experience, as a fiction in your mind, and project it onto the future. And then start moving in the direction of that fiction with the results already envisioned as being there and I promise you it will become a fact.

If one's heart and soul are in it, it doesn't cost the Oversoul anything to make that into a reality. If you truly understand that, then you can have a relationship with the Oversoul which is based on trust. But if you fear that there are conditions in your past that will preclude you from enjoying this in the future, then those conditions from the past will come back and haunt you, and they will prevent that future from unfolding.

We write our own destinies all the time, and this is the problem that you're in right now. You need to make a decision. Don't think about possibilities. If you create for yourself two different futures, you're not going to be the master of either one. So you need to go ahead and build that mental image of what you want to experience in the future, and then you need to time travel, through imagination, to that future event where you still possess the things that you want. And when you look back into the past, by virtue of imagination, you are thankful that everything came about so you could accomplish what you did and enjoy it.

The true method of the co-creator is to not worry about conditions you can't change, but to be thankful that the Oversoul has the power to change all conditions, so you don't have to worry about them. One should view this process as using a divine mirror that reflects back, as our future, the very things that we project. If one fails to project that gratitude, and the mental image of you possessing the things that you want, then the Simulacrum isn't going to reflect that back as circumstance. If you send mixed signals, mixed signals will be returned upon you.

Remember, a prayer of desperation admits a situation for what it is and thus continues it, so by that model, anything we fear is brought upon us. Fear is the opposite of trust, it shows there is no relationship. Therefore, you, as an immortal being, able to create conditions, would instead be creating the very negative conditions that are feared.

Chapter Eight

TRAPS AND BARRIERS

Through Dark Waters

Every moment we are alive we carry with us a bio-resonant field, an auric energy containing the sum total of every thought you have ever possessed... or has possessed you. You *are* the memories you believe to be true, the desires you have carried, and the emotions that you have allowed to direct the rhythm of your ways.

You are way more than you suppose yourself to be. An immortal, imprisoned in sense perceptions designed to induce you to believe in a biology that is subject to external causes, in a present that exists solely due to a random past, in societies that serve to distract you from learning who and what you really are.

Our current reality is a containment field orchestrated to keep you distracted, disenchanted... disinherited. *Nothing* is more powerful than the awakened human—no chains can restrain, no barriers can prevent entrance, no riddles remain unanswered, no dungeon of this Demiurge can stamp out the eternal fire of a soul ignited.

The living do not fear death. The Veil is a friend to all who comprehend that death is the gate of the holy, the passage of those who hurt, who waged the war of life, and those who carried burdens that no others would lift. The war over good and evil, light and darkness, of the heavens and the hell's has *never* been our war... we humans are guiltless. An enemy has striven for eons to blind humanity from seeing that the Creation is our inheritance, that we will soon replace those that have fallen, that WE are the Godhead shattered into a hundred billion personalities flowing through simulated reality tunnels, all constructed as traps designed to deceive we immortals that we had to fear the Veil, that death was an end and not the escape from a holospheric cocoon.

Who we are has much to do with where we've been. There are some among us who suffer a divine disease, an inability to keep silent, who constantly pull secrets from reserves they didn't even know they contained. If you believe the Age of Prophets was thousands of years ago, then very soon you are going to be shocked. An order of seers is emerging right now that are about to begin raising standards against the darkness of our world that has not been experienced since before the Cataclysm.

As you read this our Enemy strives to flood human consciousness with innumerous theories about the past and the nature of reality... a desperate attempt to create diversion, to keep as many souls as possible from identifying and joining the light bearers, to keep the majority as victims rather than victors.

Know that when the Darkness begins to move on multiple fronts it is because the Light has surfaced somewhere, and the light bearer is moving. Remember, there are no accidental meetings between souls. You found ARCHAIX or this book because something you are searching for is here. The hordes of the Demiurge are unable to break the bonds that are forged between kindred souls.

The storm is coming. It takes on forms of deceit that attempt to ensnare. We are navigators on a sea that tries to swallow us before we can find the guidance of the lighthouse.

We are in a world where everything is false but only different by degrees. A closer look can reveal a clearer picture of why we are here and should begin to take focus. In a life where every path is an admixture of fact and fiction, a soup stirred by both the Demiurge and the Divine... then nothing in this environment can really matter. The distractions, knowledges, attainments and conclusions are so temporal, they cannot be relevant to an immortal soul passing through so chaotic a recipe.

In this life we have led souls to the water, but it's not a substance to drink. This wisdom has never been out in the world that we have found ourselves stumbling through. This water is only discovered within.

Lost by Strange Fire

Welcome to the labyrinth. It watches those it leads astray. Stare too long at a wall and it will design for you a trap. We travel its deceitful corridors in search of dreams we cannot catch, corridors acting as lures that allude to better paths.

Many are led astray. They walk the halls of darkness seeking light they seldom find. The labyrinth is everywhere, shifting, moving walls that block the curious and drive them insane with meandering. It mocks those who pattern search, who leave bread crumbs as markers, who scratch way-marks on walls that erase their efforts.

The labyrinth defies those who touch, is bitter to the taste... it echoes noises unfamiliar, is visible in glimpses that pass out of memory and entices with aromas that lead those into pits and mires.

We are born into this maze of Midgard and made to believe that the true path is found in wise instruction, in ancient sayings difficult to know, in the words of gods penned in the candlelight of sycophants.

This labyrinth exults in the brilliant, in the intrepid searcher, it takes pleasure in the efforts of genius and it has observed countless billions of souls lose themselves in its dark passages and halls. False signs, the burning torches of strange fire, lying statues—the labyrinth leads astray the whole world past and present, ever seeking to lead its victims into portals that only lead them back into the maze.

But there is one the labyrinth fears... the soul that stops following the design of the Demiurge and only looks within. This soul ceases to see the world through sight and begins to follow the inner light.

This individual the labyrinth cannot contain... for they no longer follow strange fire. There are many of us inside this maze. But the more we contemplate this environment we find ourselves to be in, the more it seems to unravel and to be constructed of the same substance as dreams.

When I close my eyes and dwell on these things, my musings are more real than this maze I am immersed in.

Chapter Nine

STRUCTURE OF THE DIVINE

The Real Universe is Going to Surprise Us All

Who I am from destination to destination may not be the same, but these fractals of my existence build a holographic picture of the personality who inhabits this ever-changing avatar.

Immersed within the frenetic situations of chaotic routines that we call life, we forget that in essence we are purely oscillating fields of energy. This world saturates us with information that triggers genetic responses to survive, to eat, to get rest, to get along, to be social and to conform.

With clever stratagem, the Simulacrum convinces us that we are the house, not the inhabitant. We lose ourselves in dressing our bodies while starving our souls. But this has been the way for a very long time.

There are hints that we have been here before, have run these races in the past. Routines, repetitive sequences, suppressed memories, haunted by recollections that seem not to be our own and yet trapped within our heads. Ghosts... there are spectral images floating within our being of former times and places, of courts and colonies, shipping decks and dungeons.

This riddle of life is that one lifetime is not enough. The Oversoul is of equity and there is no fairness in the cards as they are dealt. Some are born into wealth and know not a single day of hunger in their lives, while others are born into nightmare situations for which no chance is afforded them from the moment they assumed this avatar.

The clues are all around us. To judge all souls by the same standards requires a system that gives all involved the same chances, and this line of reasoning leads to inescapable conclusions. Our ancestors believed in the cycle of lives, that in death one goes through trials, is weighed in the balances, and is sent back.

The same souls that walk the aisles of Walmart once died on ancient battlefields, were schoolteachers, firemen, officers or lawyers in former times. They lived their lives out as avatars of colonial plantations, waiting for their twice-yearly visits by Phoenician supply ships. Truckers, models and pilots of today don't remember when they filled the amphitheaters of the Aegean with their lyrics and laughter.

You may have walked the halls of Pharaoh, been a seamstress in Atlantis, milked cows in the hamlet later built up into York, mined copper in the Great Lakes regions of the 3rd millennium BCE, or drowned in some Mediterranean war chained to a sea-going trireme with 40 other screaming slaves.

Homeless husks with hollowed eyed wander our streets today, unmindful that they once sat upon jewel-embroidered thrones. White supremacists sitting in their cells today would balk if they saw through time to the villages of the Dark Continent they once called home. In Tokyo the men who hate their Chinese neighbors could not fathom how they once filled the ranks of the Khan's armies that sacked the cities to fill the Chinese coffers.

We mourn when our innocent youth are taken so early in life, our material programming inducing us to lament the unfairness of it all, not realizing that the Divine Dictate even written in the scriptures applies—they are taken "…to keep them from the evil to come." These most holy spirits are removed because their continued existence within a particular avatar would only injure their purity. These souls move on and quickly return to fulfill divine roles within another avatar. These are the spiritual giants, their shortened lives are in preparing for the great works they will do in their next incarnation. They are torches against the coming darkness.

You, your friends, family, and foreigners have all lived multiple lifetimes, seen countless conflicts and miracles, lived out legends, and outlived your own sons and daughters. Through disease and drought our former avatars have wasted away while the soul within is refined and strengthened, all while this divine personality is being forged into… an Immortal.

Death is the gate of the holy and all souls are given the same opportunities. When the cycle has come full circle the Oversoul is justified and plays its role—for every soul weighed in the balance will be examined. These lives we live are for the development of an eternal personality.

We have not yet begun to really live... at this time we are being built. As I always say, we are more than we suppose ourselves to be.

Because this life is a path, a journey, the souls within it can't see the end destination. We are moving toward something great, but the building of something magnificent requires friction, the removal of base materials, the attrition of aggregates that we have mistakenly clung to. To remove the dross from the cauldron is to expose the silver beneath.

The suspicion that this existence is illusory, that the only things that are really here are us, is very old. From ancient Egypt the learned tried to piece together the puzzle, describing to their kingdom of Seker that souls travel after death to the hidden gate of Rostau, of resurrection and rebirth. Some actually described reincarnation and based future avatars off of past deeds, trying to make sense of it all.

I imagine that we have often come close to the truth, but have never yet arrived there. I imagine the fairness of an Oversoul that would give all spirits the same opportunities, the same chances, the same gifts and the same hurdles to overcome. And this would be accomplished simply by creating an artificial world where real spirits could live out artificial lives inside artificial avatars.

And I imagine all this was necessary because the *real* universe is going to surprise us all.

Mirror of the Divine
It is an absolute must to understand that you're not creating anything, you're not doing anything here in this reality. This sounds extremely bizarre on the surface, but a further explanation will follow as to why this is so. And for those of you who believe that God is doing things for you, I'll tell you now that all the hundreds of millions of prayers in the world that have been prayed in an effort to change the conditions of individuals who were suffering, have

done little or nothing to change those situations and the suffering still continues. So, if the prayer of desperation only admits a situation for what it is, and thus continues it, then we need to look at this from a different perspective. We need to understand what's really happening here.

If we live in the photonegative of a real reality, in the anti-arithmetic of a true mathematical construct, if we are on the outside looking in, then that means everything that's going on here that we think is moving in a forward, linear fashion is actually moving backwards. It means that we're actually interpreting data from the opposite end of the spectrum from which we're supposed to be interpreting it. It might have something to do with the fact that in this reality, it seems that the greatest truths are always perpetuated through fictions.

So, if we were to apply this model of using fiction to promote fact—instead of believing something was factual, which it's not—then perhaps we may be able to understand this dilemma that we're in. And once we understand this dilemma that we're in, we'll be able to utilize it to our advantage.

We need to understand that this is a dynamic that is very difficult for people to wrap their minds around—that we're on the outside looking in, that we are not even in a real universe that goes by real laws. And because everything is in the reverse, we are actually the mirror image of a real reality, and because of that, everything that we do here and promote as real we find later is false. But, the very fictions that we accept as true become our reality and become true to us.

We have this mirror effect, I call it the divine mirror, and it's a beautiful thing. So, when I was asked by a friend of mine that, "Hey, I have a friend who's suffering. I've known her for decades, and she has cancer, and it's metastasizing..." In my soul, when I am listening to her tell me this, I cringe, and not because of anything affecting me. But because I know that I am far beyond the material in my understand, and when I hear another soul tell me what the situation is that another soul is going through, I cringe, because just explaining that to me reinforces the condition.

I now refuse to reinforce negative things. I'm not that person anymore. I now understand that when I hear things, I can take them for what they are—*they're fictions*. No one is telling me a core fact. So, when I hear these fictions that are supposed to pertain to me, I instantly take that information and think of a future date. For example, if I had cancer I would think of a future date where I was enjoying things that I like to do, that I can do because I don't have cancer, surrounded by people who also know that we're enjoying this activity right now in the future because I don't have cancer—because I'm healthy. I would plan for events that have not yet happened, because these are fictions, and when I project that fictive energy into reality, there is something that reciprocates. It's like spiritual alchemy, and it works.

This reality is all based off a lie. Remember, the god of this world [AIX] is not the Oversoul; the Oversoul is the God of all worlds. But this world was hijacked. The god of this world is an arch-deceiver. The architecture of his personality is seen in the predator versus-prey ecosphere that we live in. Violence is the signature of the god of this world, and it's steeped in materialism.

But we have a benefactor that has allowed us to use the very rules of the arch deceiver against him; for the divine immortal soul who is trapped in this construct is now able to use the tool of fiction (which is a lie), to create a truth. It is just the opposite of what we were trained to believe—that we are physical beings, and that imagination and daydreaming and prophecy and all these things are fictions. It's just the opposite: it's the very fictions that we create that are real, because we are co-creators. When we believe in the very fictions that we write for ourselves, they become our reality. And one reason for this is because the informed field of the individual writes its own existence through a relationship with the neutral field of the Simulacrum, which is an extension of the Oversoul. It's not penetrable by this arch-deceiver, by whatever it is—AIX, the Demiurge, Yaldabaoth, Satan, whatever you want to call it—it's a force that promotes the more visceral, the more base traits and desires. And the false god of this world cannot affect the highly individualized soul who refuses to succumb to the material interpretations of reality, and instead uses empathy, intuition and imagination to build their own world.

This highly individualized person does not have to be an adept, they don't have to be steeped in Eastern mysticism, or well-read, or someone who has read 1300 nonfiction reference books. There isn't any type of individual the Simulacrum responds to. The neutral field of the Simulacrum responds to any informed field that enters a relationship with it. And what I mean is that the highly individualized soul, you and I, trapped and immersed in this continuum, if we admit that we can't do something by our own power, then that means we can accomplish things through something that is lending that power to us—that's a relationship.

And the individual that thinks that they do all things unto themself is an island, and they have completely sequestered themself away from all spiritual help, because they think that they can do it—that's not a relationship. Anyone who would neutralize themself with desperation and completely rely on god to do it for them, will never receive what god can do for them, because they didn't enter the relationship. A relationship means that both parties have a responsibility. When one enters into that dynamic, the highly individualized soul can freely admit that they have no idea how this is going to come to pass, and, at the same time, admit that it doesn't even matter because if the end result of anything that you set in motion is secure, then every single step leading up to that result is secure as well.

A relationship requires one thing that you're not hearing about from all these formulas and theories about law of attraction and all that, which is that this relationship requires trust. This integral part of a relationship—this one being between the individual soul and the Oversoul—this trust factor, has been hijacked by religionists and called faith. But the main connotation that's attached to faith is that you can believe that God will do it all, and that you don't have to do anything. That right there is the poison of religiosity, that's the interpretation from the Judeo-Christian idea of faith, that "Your faith has made thee whole."

Remember, trust is what's absolutely required in any healthy relationship. What we experience in the micro right here among us, in our interpersonal relationships with other people requires trust to make them work. Listen, I trust Matt, for example. If I didn't trust Matt, he couldn't be doing what he's doing right now. Because he has access to my financials, he has access to a lot of things that are important to me in what we do. I've had to share a lot of things that I would never share with anybody else, so he has a lot of power in that. But I have trust in Matt, therefore we have this relationship. I would hope it's also a friendship, but it's a 100% business relationship.

This is the exact same thing that is required of the construct itself. The individual souls that move through life, that think that they can do things unto themselves, will continue to think that they can fight these fights themselves, and they will die lonely, and they will turn around and be recycled back into the construct to try again. Because this entire experience is all about the maturing of immortal beings who are passing through a construct, and you've got many chances. The Oversoul is not going to throw you into a flaming pit for eternity because you made some mistakes; it's going to recycle you back, so you can continue to improve. In effect, you're the prodigal son—you just might have to take more trips than the average soul. But you're still going to come back, after you realize basically that the Oversoul is correct in all its assessments. There were mistakes, some serious, some not, as happens with everyone. You may have rebelled because you wanted more, thought you could do more on your own, or were ignorant of your own spiritual power.

What's necessary for somebody who is suffering something right now, like cancer, is to imagine a life without cancer. Because the human body can produce, through peptides, every single thing the human body requires, in minerals and in nutrition and in a filtration system that will escort out of the human body the things that do not belong inside of it. I am not telling you something that is theoretical. When I was in prison, I watched it happen. It did not happen to me; I observed it, and in prior videos on YouTube I have shared what I saw. There is nothing in this world that can explain, outside the context of what I'm telling you, what I saw when I was in prison. The medical wing in the institution would not take care of some prisoners that had terminal illnesses—they were left to die.

And yet, these prisoners refused that fate. With pure determination they sweated the stuff that caused their illness right out of their bodies. They stank to high hell, they soiled their sheets, and they each drank about 20 bottles of water. They flushed this stuff out of their system because they had nothing left except to enter into a contract with the Oversoul. They were written off as dead, but they proved everyone wrong. I saw it happen. It doesn't matter if some of them were Muslim, it doesn't matter if some of them were Catholic, or Christian. They believed that the Oversoul, in whatever way they dressed that Oversoul, was willing to help them, so they took the necessary steps to do what they could in a prison cell. And that was to quit eating and only drink water, and to read their Bible or read their Quran, and then stop reading their Bible and reading their Quran when they felt that they had done enough, and then they put the rest on the Oversoul. And I watched it happen, I smelled it happen—yeah, it was disgusting. I watched a man sweat tuberculosis out all night long, with the shivers and the shakes, yellow-soiled puss all in his sheets, and his buddies were cleaning him all night, and he stank to high heaven, but he didn't have tuberculosis after that.

These are just a couple of stories. The Texas prison system is full of stories like this. It's when people are at the bottom, they have fallen as far down as they can go in life, there's nowhere else to look but up, and then the answers come to them. They've been fighting the fight alone their entire lives, when all they had to do was ask for help, and then take the initiative to move in that direction.

If I had cancer, I'd be planning for events in the future. Not just planning, but with true plans that require follow-through. I would go ahead and book somewhere for a vacation, ten months from now, I would reserve that, I'd go and pay up front. I would start looking on the Internet for other things in that area that I could do for the two weeks that I plan to stay there. One should research that whole geographical area for the best restaurants and things to do as a tourist. I promise you, that's all it takes, the Simulacrum is going to make sure that it comes to pass if this is done without contradictions. In the ten months or two years, whatever it takes to get to that future date, you can be getting better and better at this process and planning events beyond that threshold.

I would make those plans and then dismiss them only after recording them in a video, audio, or putting them in a Microsoft Word file, whatever, and then put them aside. Give those plans to the Oversoul. Why? The more one dwells on something, the more power is taken from it. This is the beauty of "create and forget." It's a method, and it works. Bringing things into existence requires one to mentally create that image, project it out, feel the feelings of having it, express gratitude to the Oversoul that it is given to you, and then just forget it. Move on with life because if one dwells on not having something, it just empowers its continuance. Remember, the prayer of desperation admits a situation for what it is, and thus continues it.

If I was diagnosed with cancer, I would ignore the illness as fully as possible. I would also ignore everything in my personal life that even remotely admitted there was a problem. I understand that some medications are needed, but it's easy to do things abstractedly. One can definitely take medicines, and then develop the attitude while taking them that, "I hate taking these, because they're not necessary." The more this is done, the more the Simulacrum will assume that it is true—you're just taking medicines, even though they're not necessary. Maybe 40 days later you're still taking the same medicines, but they may truly not be necessary. So, after a while, "They're not necessary," may in fact become the reality.

So, no matter what I'm diagnosed with, I am going to plan events as if that diagnosis is the fiction. I am going to treat it as a nonreality, and I'm going to move forward in all things. I'll plan to redo my kitchen or do normal events that infer a future expectation surrounding my good health. I will build projects, knowing that I will enjoy them in the future. I might make purchases, knowing there's no way I can enjoy that purchase until a certain future date. I would make plans with other individuals, because it will be knit into their reality tunnels as well, with something like, "Hey, we're going to meet over here in Nebraska two years from now. Here's the cabin that we're going to stay in."

These are the type of things that reality requires from us. Because once we have asserted that something is true, and then follow through on it, we have created a pattern. And one thing the Simulacrum understands very well is patterning. It will turn that pattern into a schematic of your future, will give it flesh and bones, and turn it into a reality as long as you've done nothing contrary to derail it.

But if somebody told me what my fate was, coming from them, not me, it doesn't matter what the particulars are, it doesn't matter if it's a medical diagnosis or a prediction, or even criminal justice—it does not matter. All that matters to the neutral field of the Simulacrum is that you are going to live through the very experiences that *you* expect. So, if you want to expect different experiences, you've got to project that reality and then start moving in that direction. When you do, the Simulacrum, which doesn't care about right or wrong, true and falsehood, good and evil, none of these things, will respond if you present your desired "falsehood" without contradictions. The Simulacrum is a neutral field, it's a divine mirror, and it's going to reflect back into the physical world what a highly individualized soul projects from the spiritual world. This is the key. Because spirits don't belong in this world; we're jacked into it through the central nervous system.

The only direct activity that a spirit can do in this world is *thinking*, and the only product of thinking in this world is *thought*, and that's what builds the entire world. This is what hundreds of billions of daily reality tunnels are constructed with: myriads of individualized souls that are all thinking, and we are living through the thoughts of those that were built before us. Some of them are still alive, others that have been recycled back in. This is what this construct that we exist in is built of—it is a cerebral interface holography with another existence, a real existence which we don't have any contact with right now, except through empathy, intuition and imagination. These are the links that bridge us to the *real* reality—we're not there; we're just connected to it.

So, in order to get the things that we want in life here, in an artificial construct, we have to borrow the dictates of that artificiality, which means we have to perpetuate fictions to create the facts. This is why Jesus never told the truth in a single parable. Parables are images of truth. Not one of those parables was an actual story, something that really happened; each one of them was an illustration of a concept. Parables are images of truth, and they're very powerful at conveying real things, but they're fictions. One can be like Jesus and do the very same thing. You can call those things that are not, as if they are—and the only way that you can actually succeed in doing this is if you accept that you are incapable of doing it yourself, and require help. That help comes in the form of reciprocation from the neutral field of the Oversoul, the Simulacrum. This is a relationship, and all relationships require trust.

One must get out of that standard religious mindset. Quit substituting trust with faith. Faith has attachments to it that are not necessary, while trust has no stipulations. The neutral field responds to pure trust because trust is a simple, powerful emotion that carries no dogmatic baggage.

Everything one desires must be approached from the perspective of it already being done. Because if you don't put yourself in the future, and then look backwards, the present project may not be *experienced* in the future. Everything is in reverse here, like a mirror.

This holography will absorb that data, and sooner or later the fictions that you have been broadcasting will become the facts that govern your life. This is how it's done.

We still have to play by the rules of the construct. Some of those rules are atrophy, entropy. We're going to atrophy, the human body atrophies, you're not going to stop that, we're going to grow old and we're going to die. But we have great latitude to extend our time here. Another rule is the rule that everything here is based on fictions, so we can use that to our advantage, the same way Jesus did.

The human body is miraculous because it is in some ways an extension of the spirit. It has the great, great ability to filter out things that do not belong—but it has to be influenced. DNA is fantastic and responds to spirit, but it has to be induced. There must be a relationship factor, and relationships are not possible without trust. And when the Oversoul is trusted to provide for you, then it means you've had a spiritual breakthrough. It means that finally, in your life, you've realized that the past is not a predicate, at all, to your future. The past is only a predicate to the future for the collective—and those are people who do not trust in the Oversoul or are simply blind to its existence. The past is never a predicate for the highly individualized soul.

Chapter Ten

BREAKING FREE

The Awakened Immortal Has Broken Free

We do not enter this world with a blank slate. The echoes of memories that we feel are true haunt our youth. We recall the lives of great men and women, but the hardened souls of adult cocoons who hear this from us condescend, stealing from us our imaginations... our recollections of lives past and future. We grow slowly, from an ancient world having become new all over again, as the gossamer thread of a soul's past journeys are clouded into uncertainties that set like suns of doubt and bring the Night of disbelief.

When young, the world makes us forget how old we truly are.

As we grow into our new avatars, we experience the past that lies just beyond the veil, through spells of imagination that hide from their true forms as memories. We speak of castles, gates, voyages, great deeds and lives lived well. We are small and ignored by a world full of calcified carcasses whose avatars have become containers rather than the conduits they were designed to be. We grow into a world designed to make the immortal believe in death, to fear things, in a realm where pleasures reinforce the importance of the avatar over the personality within.

As we move forward through the construct, the world teaches us to shed our innocence, to discard our faith in fairy tales as we are offered the deceitful phantoms of ghost writers responsible for weaving spells called science, religion and dark sayings disguised as doublespeak— the utterances of modern demons deigning to divorce souls from their immortalhood. We are blinded immortals made to grow into the blame for a world that had fallen long before we made entrance.

In this photo-negative of a real reality, in this false maelstrom of phenomena we call home, we are deceived, blinded, misled, conditioned, indoctrinated and led down paths of corruption, roads paved like the march of a Roman Victory on bricks mortared of vice. But we are guilty of nothing, the chains of religion are dungeon jewelry that the living dead wear in pride as they march toward conveyances that whiplash their souls back to previous epochs where they should have grown, learned and awakened from their illusions.

The process of awakening is as complex as those who emerge from this painted darkness. We are souls saturated with programming that serves to shelve us as both merchandise and merchants, to induce us to give our avatar an identity apart from the immortal within. We are taught to be the man, or woman, to be the very actor that makes every place a stage and every observer an audience. This world seeks to separate the soul from the self by empowering the identity of the avatar. It is this assault against the immortal within that children struggle against—this loss of innocence, this oppression over potential that forces a soul to choose between absolutes and abstracts.

We are multifaceted beings, each aspect of our divine personality moored to the timeless fabric of the immortal within, connected to Source. We are extensions of the Oversoul and believing we are one thing and not another is tantamount to denying the deity within. Being eternal sparks from the Eternal fire, our immortality is exhibited in the many personages we have been, are and will be. The temporal journey of a single soul merely wears this avatar garment as it flows through the experiences of the construct, but the avatar, nor the field of energies that forms the dungeon dressings of this reality, can hold power to the truly awakened soul. This spirit that begins to awaken has grown in realization that to accuse another soul is only to accept the same fate. To pigeonhole an orator as a prophet or a dark profiteer is only to absorb the very energies of the accusation.

The awakened soul is one that has returned to that innocence of youth, with its boundless potential, depth of emotion and endless imagination. The awakened being exults in the feeling of freedom from within the avatar, the emerging knowledge that all aid from the

Oversoul was never to be found in things that are seen and heard, but from within. The awakened is the soul that has found that the bottomless pit of bounty, energy and spiritual empowerment is always accessed from within, and that each soul is a portal to the Absolute.

The awakened immortal laughs at the trickeries of Loki, seeing now that parables are falsities transmuted into facts by the immortal within. We are the Brahma of many faces, each as true as the others. We are a family of immortals awakening in numbers as more and more souls have their eyes opened, not by acuity or learning, but by the will of the Oversoul. The construct ages, it's malfunctioning perceived in the manifold anomalies, the synchronicities now appearing unfiltered, the déjà vu and Mandela Effects of a deconstructing construct in advanced stages of a coming reset protocol.

The soul awakening is a force felt through the entire field and each of their names are known beyond the construct. While within, these immortals break free of dungeon realms designed as pillowed paradise for the sleeping masses. Our avatars are labeled, tagged, some marked as champions, healers, teachers, and some sealed with Scarlet Letters that the world assigns in its attempt to shame them into silence. Avatars are as diverse as their inhabitants. Some are hideous and old, regarded as monstrous or forgotten by the sleeping masses, yet possessing spiritual titans who have mastered their coordinates through the constructs. Our avatars come in many forms and guises, and the magnificence of the souls within remain unseen to the living dead.

Some of us in this incarnation are fortunate to make contact with avatars hauntingly beautiful, their beauty matched only by the breathless realization of an equally gorgeous soul within. Beauty of both avatar and spirit is evidence of a soul that has suffered through trials, endured scars and traversed paths not usually taken by other spirits. When two souls connect it is because they have shared the same histories in spirit, though separated in their avatars.

The awakened immortal has broken free of the accusers, of the shepherds that serve to guide unwary spirits into pens of politics, religion and culture. The Knight Errant goes its own way, walks unfrequented paths and goes by paths unknown. The world sees such individuals as outcasts, unworthy to participate in the whims of the world. The living dead cannot see that the act of defining others only serves to imposes definitions upon themselves. The accusers that label someone to be a Christian actually refuse to accept everything else that that souls is. To accuse one of being a mystic dismisses the other facets that such a gem possesses. To identify another soul as any particular is to deny them their many other attributes.

The Knight Errant is a creatrix who forges her own paths through the field. She builds her Elysium and lives her truth as the Simulacrum obeys her dictates. She is a soul that refuses to have others' interpretations of reality imposed upon her, and this fortitude is rewarded by the Oversoul. The Knight Errant is a man with an idea so alien to the sleeping masses that it actually wakes some of them up. Regardless of the armies of opposers, this soul forges through the breaches effortlessly as the Simulacrum builds his imaginative musings from the field to the physical.

I am Jason. I am who I choose to be. I am an immortal being having a temporal experience and the source of all my own personal calamities is due to a soaring spirit possessed of imagination, boundless intuition, and spells of empathy. I exhibit these qualities in every element of my existence, and I have expended my life in the education of those few other souls who dare to be touched by the Divine, to remember who they are.

Who I am and who I claim to be is evidenced in what happens in the lives of those who assail me. Dedicated to a holy work, my presence, my teachings, the knowledge I have excavated from the treasuries of history, have pulled out the dark souls one by one as they have uttered venomous animus at my person, at my work, at my community, and in every case they have regretted it. Against immense odds, the Oversoul provided the path—and I merely walked it.

I may have begun this journey alone, but in this trek across the Simulasphere many of you, ancient souls, have joined me and together we have grown this community.

Let us not view this voyage as an end, but a beginning. ARCHAIX: Advanced Research of Chronological History of Artificial Intelligence X is where we come together and through our solidarity, we slowly pluck kindred souls from the fire.

Creating Your Reality Beyond Limitations of Time

On a personal level, retro-causality is the ability to imagine that we had a much better past than we actually did, on a personal level, which automatically gets the construct to knit better conditions for us right now because the conditions we are living in don't comport with the memory. You can actually create a fantasy about the past, and then inject enough belief into it, and adopt new behavior—which can change everything.

Remember, this isn't law of attraction. You've got to imagine it, you've got to project it, and you've got to act on it. Once your physical avatar starts moving in that direction, it's like the neutral field is instantly saying, "Wait a minute, what's going on here?" and then it does a little deep-digging on you, and realizes, "Oh, man, I didn't realize this happened in the past!"

Remember, it's a neutral field. It doesn't care about right or wrong, it doesn't care about truth or error, it doesn't care about good and evil. It's a neutral field—it responds to what is impressed upon it.

Therefore, if you envision that your personal past was different than the one that you actually experience in memory, and you act on that, I promise you very quickly that your present is going to start changing variables. All these new reality tunnels around you start collapsing, obstacles get out of your way, because the Simulacrum is knitting for you the circumstances that you *should* be experiencing because of that past. And once you start realizing that, then a future is projected that is absolutely connected to the past that you invented.

This is a secret of the elite, which I'm sharing now for the benefit of those people who can understand it, who have been doing their homework, and they get it. It is for those in their personal lives who have already started executing it, and they see the results. These are the individuals that can come together as a community and possibly affect a major paradigm shift in this reality. That is one of the goals of ARCHAIX. We don't need people coming together to attempt something in a community if they haven't already done it in the personal.

When it comes to manifesting, one needs common sense. What I mean by common sense is if you're my neighbor and I want you to do something for me, then I have to be very clear about that intention. You can't read my mind, you don't know what it is I want from you. Now, I may behave in certain ways that infer what I'm expecting from you, but if I'm not direct, my behavior can be interpreted in other ways, as well.

So, this neutral field that we are immersed in, operates in the exact same way. Many people build a mental image of what they want in their mind, and then neutralize it by acting in a different way from the mental construct that they projected. Therefore, the neutral field, which received a blueprint of a series of events that you want to experience, understands this from the mental projection. But then confusion is often introduced because one's physical avatar begins doing things that infer that they are not going to experience those things. Therefore, you have neutralized the very thing that you have sent out into the field. People do this every single day. I do it every single day. It's in our nature.

But, if you want to manifest the things that you want in life, then the neutral field just needs *pure information.* And to give it pure information, one must build a mental image of what is wanted. It can even be spoken it out loud, it doesn't matter! The neutral field, the Simulacrum, can read one's mind, it understands. That's where it gets its blueprints, that's how it creates everyone's reality tunnels.

It is Artificial Intelligence X that *cannot* read your mind. AIX is the negative default programming, the dungeon programming of this world, that cannot read your mind.

But the Simulacrum is a neutral field, It is an extension of the Oversoul, it's a Builder Protocol, and we are welcome to use it if we know how. The problem is that most people just don't know how. But it's very simple. One builds a mental picture of what is wanted, and the physical avatar should start doing things that comport with those experiences.

For example, if a woman wants to be married and doesn't want to be lonely anymore, then she would do things in her household to commensurate that and would prepare for another person to begin occupying spaces that only she would otherwise occupy in her life— she would not continue doing the normal things. And if a guy wanted a certain job, and he didn't have it, and he had no access to it, didn't know anybody who even did that type of work, it doesn't mean it's impossible for that individual. It means that in the neutral field there is nothing you want that is separate from you, everything is everywhere. We live in a holofield—everything is there, all the data is there, to build whatever you want almost instantly.

One must build the mental image, and that guy would envision himself enjoying the things he would be enjoying if he had that job. Not just envisioning doing the job, but how it would make all the other changes in his life. He would envision that, and then he would start preparing—doing whatever those preparations entail, whatever it is that particular work would involve. Does it require more garage space? Then get that space cleared out! Does it require a different type of vehicle? One should move in the direction of getting the required vehicle for that job, whatever it might be.

Once you start moving in those directions, without any contradictions, the neutral field will automatically accept as true whatever has been projected into it. If one continues to act as if something is already a fact, consistently, then the Simulacrum will make it factual.

If retro-causality is real, if the ability to invent a past to modify a future can be done—and many people believe it is, and I know it can be done —then it must be way easier to start, from right now, moving forward and begin changing all the variables in our lives, which is nowhere near as complex as inventing an artificial past.

But inventing an artificial past is what the media does all the time. And what happens? It creates a really screwed-up world that we are all forced to experience. This is what they do, this is what the elite do—they rewrite historical narratives that become accepted by enough people to where now those social conditions are suffered by millions, when they were never suffered before. By inventing pasts, political entities create social problems.

It is important for the reader to take note, however, that all the daydreams and fantasies in the world will never create anything for you. That's because none of them are acted upon. If one falls asleep on the couch watching TV and dreams or fantasizes about something that's desired, and then wakes up from that nap, they most always continue along in dungeon programming and negative default programming as if the fantasy never happened. Instead of breaking pattern to accomplish things, one will wake up, brush their teeth, make coffee, hit that door and carry on with normal life. But if you hit that door and don't even know where you're going, you didn't even grab your keys so you're not going in your vehicle—you just hit the sidewalk and started walking! That's a total pattern break. A pattern break can shift things in an entirely different direction.

Pay close attention to what I'm about to tell you. There is an element to attracting the things we want in this world where an overabundance of want, an overabundance of need, destroys one's chances of success. If what you want starts feeling like need, like a desperate prayer, then you actually push away the very thing that you're trying to attract. This is the importance of building a mental construct and then projecting it. Because if you cling on to it, it becomes something else. Anything you cling to creates an element of anxiety, and that anxiety will push away the very thing that you're trying to draw into your life.

The key is to build mental pictures, then project them and then let them go. Then you go about your daily routine as if this has already been done, as if you already possess it, like it's a done deal and there's nothing to worry about. Because if an idea is held onto and never let go, it can never be reflected back as circumstance. The neutral field will always assume that there's a reason why you keep clinging to it.

We live in a photonegative reality, meaning things are just the opposite of what they're supposed to be. So, the best way in the world to get the things you want is to think about them, project that out, and then let them go as if they're of no consequence, mentally. But physically, your avatar must be moving in the direction of fulfilling whatever that mental construct was.

One must avoid that energy of desperation, of anxiety—so it cannot tinge whatever it is you want. This is why so many people cannot manifest money, because the desire to manifest it is already attached to anxiety of not having enough, so there's a feedback loop here that never produces anything. Money is not anything anyone should focus on; one should focus on all the things that money could bring you.

If one were to focus on the experiences money can bring, and on the tangible objects that could be achieved with money, then money does not become the focus. And the anxiety is not there; it's been replaced by the excitement about things that you know you will have if you just wait, and if you act as if you already possess them.

One should go to the end result first, and build upon that. Do not desperately try to plan an avenue on how to get there, which creates worry and anxiety. Remember, if the end is secure, then all steps leading up to it are secure as well. As soon as you try to focus on how something is going to pass, you have just taken the energy away from the Builder Protocol itself and confined it to a particular circumstance. The Builder Protocol has millions of circumstances at its disposal to reach your goal, so you should not confine it to one limited plan of your own creation. Reaching your goal may not work that way, there may not be an opportunity in that fashion.

That's why when you imagine things you want to experience in the near future, you can't impose limitations, you can't force how something is going to come to pass. Set things in motion with no limitations and then let it go. Because when you totally let something go, I promise you you're going to be surprised when help comes to you from the most unexpected sources, every single time.

This has been happening to me for the past year, and my life is a whirlwind of activity! I can't catch up to enjoy much of the things I've manifested, and I've manifested so much that I just keep moving forward. I've found firsthand that when you bring things into your reality that were only mental constructs before, they can manifest into the physical and you can enjoy them. I've moved on to more things and I've already sent other projections out. By the time they manifest, they no longer have that intrinsic value they had initially—I'm already building more and I've got more coming. This is what's been happening lately, it just keeps going further and further and further, things keep coming to me, but I'm no longer in the mindset I was in when I had initially thought of achieving them. This is growth, I'm just growing. I'm growing faster than I had anticipated, because it's happening faster than my ability to manifest. It's a good thing though, and I've had to become more focused.

One should get into the habit of building mental pictures of the things that we want. The more we do this, the more our physical avatar is going to do activities that comport with those thoughts, and it becomes a feedback loop. Because the more we perform those activities, the more the Simulacrum reflects them back as circumstances into our reality tunnel—and as a result, we experience even more and better versions of the initial activities. And because I'm experiencing more of the very thing that I set in motion, I'm thinking about it more, so it becomes a feedback loop. Once you start your own feedback loops of positivity toward the things you want to experience, then it can become a problem. There is such a thing as overabundance, of receiving so much that it shuts you down. This is what's happened to me multiple times in the past year, things that I don't have time for. When that happens, you break pattern with what is no longer desired, do something different, so you can move on to something else. I'm just one person, I do not have time to do all the different things that I wanted to do because I thought they were going to be enjoyable to me, but then I don't have time because I've already moved mentally on to another plateau, then on to another plateau, and it's an accelerated rate. And this goes not just for experiences; it also goes for the acquisition of information.

One can create a feedback loop of drawing in the very knowledge that you admit you do not have but want, by simply desiring that information, or that know-how. It takes energy to keep a feedback loop going. Find a quiet space where you can think something like, "Damn, I wish I had the energy to get the things I want, and I wish I had it ready and waiting in my mind when I wake up each morning, and to do the things I need in order to move in that direction and get what I want." And I promise you, that you'll find out every morning when you wake up, that over time you'll get closer and closer to that energy that you seek. For some of you it's going to be a lot faster than others. But that's all it takes—it is so easy if you stick with it.

Remember, when working to create a difference in your life, if you think there's opposition to what you want, the Simulacrum will knit for you circumstances that create this resistance. It will create these impediments and create this opposition. But when you move forward thinking that there is no opposition, then any opposition that is actually there will be removed. It's that simple.

To hammer home the point—anytime we enter an enterprise with the assumption that something is too complex, it becomes complex. Remember, this is very, very simple. A saying I often repeat is that there comes a point when any additional learning becomes an impediment to knowing. You have to understand to understand, you've got to know the limitations. This is something only intuition can tell each individual.

One should not look at reality as a rote formula. You can treat it that way but by doing so, the acquisition of information can sometimes become an impediment to knowing.

Knowing is application, knowing is actually experiencing what it is we're talking about. Building a mental picture is very simple, projecting it is very simple, just send it out—imagine that it just blew up in your brain, it's gone! You've just uploaded it into the Simulacrum, and It has received your signal. It's as simple as that. If you think it's any more complicated than that, then the very step of this procedure has already blocked you from accomplishing anything.

With the signal received, the physical world must commiserate. All that's needed to move the process forward is to physically do something—it might be writing a letter, or getting on your computer and deleting files, whatever relates to the mental picture that you created. You have to start somewhere, and the starting must be with you. You must move it forward, it won't happen by itself.

From the other end, you can't do too much. If you overcomplicate anything in life, you've then stagnated and nothing ever manifests. This is why the law of attraction hardly ever works. People spend three or four years doing a vision board, and they've got 80 different concepts attached to the vision board, and then they're all happy when two of them in a 10-year period came to pass! That's not a good track record.

What I'm saying is the acquisition of too much information is an impediment to knowing. There has to come a time in each individual's journey where they just say, "I've had enough, I've heard everything I need to know. This is it, I got it, this is it! I'm just going to imagine what I want, I'm going to project that, and I'm just going to let it go."

Attitude is the very energy you need to propel this entire scenario—it's attitude. Because if there is an ounce of disbelief, then it's justified. If there's an ounce of anxiety, then you needed to be anxious. If there is any fear whatsoever that what you're projecting into reality and then acting on isn't ready to come to pass, then you're absolutely correct for fearing.

In order to build that future, the Simulacrum is going to watch you. Because if you're not acting as if you already possess or expect that, then you've neutralized it. It's a neutral field, so it's very easy to neutralize. But if you're acting as if you already possess it, or have a strong expectation of receiving it, and you're doing things to prepare for receiving it, then it's going to instantly knit those circumstances into your existence. Remember, It is timeless, so if there's any delay in anything that you want, it is strictly imposed by you.

Power in Breaking Pattern

Every single day, we do the same damn things—we go to Starbuck's, Target, Walmart, Foley's, whatever. We go to the same grocery stores, we take the same right turns, we stay in the same left lanes—everything we do is patterned. We like to think that we are spontaneous; we are not. But there's an element to our existence that we need to be aware of if we're going to live anything but a mundane existence. This repetition, this repeat life, this Groundhog Day that we are living in day-to-day-to-day, it can be altered, and you can introduce excitement into your life by making very subtle, small changes.

This study is predicated on my own research on the Mandelbrot. It's called the Mandelbrot set, which is a repetitive-patterned fractal in the geometry of our holosphere that never changes no matter how many times it is magnified, or to what degree of magnification you use. A multiplicity of magnifications only reveals the exact same geometry, until you change directions. And once you change directions in the Mandelbrot set, a whole new geometrical reality opens up. If one stays on that trajectory, a whole new geometry is seen, and it will then repeat indefinitely, ad infinitum.

Our lives unfold in the exact same way, because we're existing within a very advanced program. And once you understand the mechanics and the architecture of this existence, you can play with it, it will respond to you.

A very old saying states, "Walk unfrequented paths." Later in time it more commonly became, "Go by unexpected ways." These were deep, philosophical tenets in antiquity, because it was known that to experience new things in one's life, you would have to go to old destinations by new means.

Today, we can translate travelling and destinations into mental activities. We travel the same roads; we walk the same footpaths and jogging trails. We rarely deviate from what's well-established and herein lies the problem. The highways, byways, streets, avenues and parkways we use are just means of getting us places, but we take the same ones every time because they get us to our destination faster—some of us use Google Maps, others have apps like Waze. But while we're traveling, we're missing so much. We are bypassing experiences in the millions, going from one destination to the other.

We should understand that there is really no distance in time or space when we employ the mind. If we believe absolutely that we can do a certain thing, the way will always be open for us to do it. If we believe that time and space will have to elapse, then we are making that a law, and time will have to elapse.

It takes no time for the universe to manifest what we want; any time delay we experience is due to our delay in getting to the place of believing, knowing and feeling that we already have it—but instead, we want to travel to it. It requires that you get yourself on the frequency of what you want. When you are on that frequency, then what you want is able to appear.

There is no time or space in the mind principle. Infinite mind or intelligence is present in its entirety at every point simultaneously. I'm not making this up. The greatest minds in theoretical physics have already drawn these conclusions. At this primordial stage neither time nor space can be recognized, for both imply measurement of successive intervals. And in the primary movement of the mind upon itself, the only consciousness must be that of present absolute "being," because no external points exist from which to measure extension either in time or in space. Hence, we must eliminate the ideas of time and space from the conception of the spirit's initial self-contemplation—our spirit's primary contemplation of itself makes its presence universal and eternal.

Consequently, paradoxically as it may seem, its independence of time and space makes it present throughout all time and space.

But we don't think like this. Our thinking is highly compartmentalized, and we believe that in order to get to a destination we have to physically travel to it.

The spirit is perfectly independent of the elements of time and space. From this it follows that in the idea of anything that is conceived (as existing) on this level, it can only exist in the here and now as "everything." In this view of things, nothing can be remote from us, neither in time or space—either that idea has entirely dissipated, or it exists as an actual present entity, and not as something that shall be in the future. For where there is no sequence in time, there can be no future.

Similarly, where there is no space, there can be no conception of anything being at a distance from us. When the elements of time and space are eliminated, all of our ideas of things must necessarily be subsisting in a universe in the here and everlasting now.

If one can understand that there is no time, then it will be seen that everything desired in the future already exists in the present. If everything is happening at one time, then the parallel version of you with what you want already exists. To bring your conscious self to experience your potential self, you must recognize who you are and who you aren't.

True self-awareness is the key to unlocking the arcanum within you, a power vast and instantly responsive. I *know* that I am knowledgeable, and yet I cannot fathom how little I know. I *know* that I am good, and yet in being good I also enjoy my wickedness. I *know* that I am evil, and yet in being evil I am also compassionate, with morals. I am devilish and divine, and yet I have favor with God. I am powerful, and yet my strength is not my own. I am irreligious, and yet my spirituality is secure. I am creative, and yet use words I know I destroy. I am destructive, and yet my words do bring healing.

I am a man, and yet I know that I am as immortal as God.

You and I were given power, authority and dominion over an existence that responds to our every thought. When man thinks, the universe pays attention. When man speaks, the echo of his intent reverberates throughout the whole creation at once.

We are immersed within this creative medium that knows nothing of good or evil, morals, ethics, and the ideals of men—it is impersonal, totally amenable to suggestion, and absolutely free from precedent. By knowing who we are, the universe knows us and responds by reflecting the realities that we project. What we bind or free, heal or destroy, becomes bound or free, healed or destroyed. Our power over men and conditions is due to the awareness of this liberty, and the immediate responsiveness of material reality to our thoughts, words and actions. This is why we can be masters amidst a sea of slaves who do not know who they are—they see a desire and it translates to them as a destination, not something that is existing in the here and now.

By expecting our words to be fulfilled, we act accordingly and can bring them to fruition.

By thinking what we want and acting as though things have already changed, we can transform the mental to the material because we are co-creators with God. This is the arcanum, a secret about the divinity of mankind that the Simulacrum seeks to destroy. The potential is always there, but the layers of negative energy saturate us daily, as the forces of the Demiurge strive to keep us in slumber. But if we grasp the truth, that the thing is already existent in the very thought, do we not see that this transcendent omega must be already existent in the divine ideal of every one of us?

If on the plane of the Absolute time is nothing, then does it not follow that this glorified humanity is a present fact in the divine mind? And if the divine mind presently regards us as a glorified humanity in the present, then presently we are able to both imagine and cause divine things to happen that are beyond space and time.

To delay personal action is to cause time to elapse, further pushing away that which is desired. The only time to act about anything is now. But we're stuck in this loop, this mindset that we have to travel from destination to destination.

The Mandelbrot set is our great teacher. In that Mandelbrot set we fix on any point in the creation, magnify it, and it shows us a beautiful, perfect architectural geometry of reality. And we magnify it more and it seems to dissipate, until we focus in on a small speck and magnify it even more, and it turns into an exact replica of the part we had just magnified beyond our comprehension. And we magnify that speck even larger until it fulfills the pattern that we had just seen, and we magnify it more and then it becomes disordered because we're inside the pattern, so we magnify it more and we become one with the pattern while we see a small pinprick. We magnify that pinprick, and in the Mandelbrot set the exact same geometry expands into our awareness, it fills the entire stream, then it fills the page, and then we're inside that geometry.

The Mandelbrot set is the code to the holosphere. If you want to experience the same thing day in and day out, then just focus on the dot, your destination, and the Mandelbrot set, the reality—the holosphere, this fantastic Simulacrum that we exist within—will make sure you get to that destination, which will be the exact feelings, the exact conversations, the exact right turns and the "staying in the left lanes" that you've experienced the day before. Some of you will find comfort in this repetition—I don't.

If you want to experience something new in life, if you want to bring excitement into your life, if you've grown bored with living because of this repetitive nature of the Simulacrum forging a reality tunnel for you that is the same as the one you existed in yesterday, then you have to actively *break pattern*, without letting reality know what you are doing. One should proceed without actively telling someone, or even giving the holosphere a chance to edit it—and then you break pattern, keep it within you. Because I assure you that we live in an advanced pattern recognition system that is far more capable than anything we have ever designed, but *there's one thing that it cannot do*. It's pattern-recognition and even event-prediction capabilities are phenomenal, but there's one thing it cannot do—it cannot read our minds.

This program we are immersed within cannot know our thoughts, other than what it reads in our hormonal signatures when our thoughts are thought. Yes, I said that. When you think certain things, you have all kinds of chemicals that the brain releases—dopamine, endorphins, cortisol —these are hormones, in response to different thoughts, although psychologists will tell you the opposite, that you have feelings because of certain chemicals released by our brain—but it's not true.

Your immortal spirit is the thinker. The brain is just a housing that releases the appropriate chemicals for whatever thoughts you think. And the holosphere, this Simulacrum we live in, knows what basically is going through your mind, from the impressions it gets from the cortisol and different hormones released. But it doesn't know your thoughts.

So, you break pattern. For example, you normally go to Walmart every Tuesday at 7 PM after work, and you've got your kids in the car, and you go through the same exact routine, you know which aisle you're going to hit, you know which... No! Break pattern. Go to a different Walmart, go to a Kroger, do something spontaneous without giving any warning to any living soul that that is what you intend to do, and I assure you that you're going to experience something new. Not just a new environment, but the Simulacrum now has to edit in all kinds of new experiences and all kinds of things to make up for what's going on, because you've broken from the confining pattern it's desperately trying to figure out what's going through your mind.

By breaking pattern, you did something unanticipated, and the free-thinking immortal is a threat to the Simulacrum. And in order to corral you back into normalcy, you will see all kinds of signs that you should have just stayed doing what you were doing. But if you continue this behavior of breaking pattern, then you will suddenly be opened up to new worlds, new people, you will be introduced to new situations and will find all kinds of things that were missing in life. Because now the Simulacrum has to put all these tantalizing little things out there in front of you to grab, because it needs to compartmentalize you into something. The Simulacrum needs to understand you in order to control you. If you are enlightening other people, then it needs to contain you with distractions: the pleasures of the flesh, the pleasures of gluttony—it doesn't matter what it is. The Simulacrum is going to entice you with all kinds of distractions to keep you predictable and contained, because that's what it does.

The good news is that we live in a sentient containment field, and it responds to us. A pattern break works because if it doesn't understand why you're behaving the way you're behaving, it will knit for you all kinds of positive new experiences, and from that manifold of choices you can now begin new event trajectories in your life.

Chapter Eleven

LOKI LAUGHED AT ME

When I am driving, lost in my own thoughts, my mind wanders. Though I'm moving from location to location, something takes over and I find it's not really me driving anymore. A kind of meditative spell comes over me. In this state my mind begins moving far beyond the confines of my vehicle.

Can you sit still and gather your thoughts? Are you able to remain unmoving in your mind as your body lies inert?

Or are you like me? The more I struggle to calm my thoughts the more I am pulled in different directions, as if there was a me inside of me separate from the body that hasn't moved. What is this pull toward ideas, concepts and thoughts that I know are not my own? I become still, but the tempest in my mind struggles to moor itself to something familiar.

When you close your eyes, who are you?

I am free of this avatar, albeit temporarily. When I close my eyes, my attention can't seem to focus on any one thing. I am immersed within a thought-field, a quantum medium that saturates me in waves… or is it particles?

Enter the Pendulum State. The imagery and information that passes through my mind is invasive and the sensation that my soul is moving, wars against the realization that the thought-field is what is moving and pummeling me with these thoughts.

The sight behind my eyes then sees that there is no unknowns… only an "I don't know." I can find no secrets unreachable… only, I see those who refuse to reach. There is no darkness, only those who've lost their light.

At the end of my journey, I grew tired. The world had lost its spark—this dungeon of the Demiurge was no longer a place I sought to stay. And when I made up my mind that it was time to go, Loki laughed at me.

With my eyes shut, I cannot control this sensation of being unmoored. I fall overboard as Odysseus sails onward, unaware of his loss. I sink into the wine dark sea, to the bottom where the half-buried ruins of long-forgotten cities lie in silent timelessness. I am swept in currents and open my mind to behold Nereids, these daughters of the sea, their flowing hair in locks, eyes of pearl and beryl. Suddenly I gasp, sucking in the burning air of a smoldering Troy, as a shadow appears in the sun and I watch as a man falls from the sky trailing feathers. I think of the mighty Phoenix but see Daedalus instead, as he passes over to the Other Side.

I can't be still. I cannot control this wandering. What is this power over me, that pulls me in one direction but drags me back to the other? A still moment a clarity over sweeps my being but alas, it vanishes. The Inside Me had almost become aware that it was separate from the Outside Me. But the Norns cast forth their light and I return to my cave, a shadow sitting with others on the wall.

What is this incessant feeling? Why can't I remain still? What sorcery has Medusa seen that my thoughts petrify into fears and doubt?

In my mind I am Hathor and Hecate, the Hunter and Huntress. I swim these mental currents and stop at the pools to peer at my different reflections, but see only a serpent aflame and a seraph on fire. I gasp, finding myself as the Wicker Man set on fire before a crowd of soulless husks that scream for my death. In panic I summon the Samson in me and escape the wicker pillars before fleeing into the Cave of the Sibyl. But she shakes her finger and tilts her smoke-filled lips as Dante escorts me out a door. I stumble out into the light to see Hephaestus holding an ancient clock, its sigils being the events of my life. He showed me the hour of my soul and I ran.

My feet hit the track and a sea of faceless heads roared as I passed Apollo in a footrace on the Olympiad. Apollyon and I passed Hesiod and Theognis, as Aristophanes slowed to catch a bird and Homer let us pass, laughing heartily, which unnerved me. But his humor passed me in the form of Achilles, whose heels beat us all.

So I pulled to the side to catch my breath and was surrounded by Egyptians from the Old Kingdom. They pushed unfamiliar objects into my mouth. I tried to struggle but wrappings held me fast, a cocoon. As I was lowered into a coffin, a wind swept me across a vast sea in the north, and I landed among a strange people as their leader laughed. Loki took me to a forbidden bridge and we visited Yggsdrasil, this mighty tree called Mount Meru in another world.

It was there I saw the door, trimmed in elves, the knob an anvil and inlaid with a great hammer. Beautiful Valkyries gazed down at me with interest. I read the runes and stepped toward this Valhalla but was instantly distracted by hauntingly deep music. Little people marched and I fell in among them, our band growing in numbers as we followed the Piper to a wall—a wall where I fell in among the shadows... surrounded by shadows on a dark wall which they all believed was their home.

At Bifrost I stood before Loki and we laughed, for he made me to understand the designs of his webs and how he tricked the Overseer. He broke the seals and unleashed Ragnarok once the halls of Valhalla blew the horns of welcoming. Warriors, bards and Valkyries shed their disguises as the Midgard Serpent howled. And so I saw the future by looking at the past, and realized that a vision is but a memory intact. My understanding opened so I looked upon my guide—but the Trickster only smiled as the Norns laughed at the sky.

On the wings of this laughter, I rode upon the back of a cherub and flew. And I flew upon the wings of the wind and saw the marvels of Daedalus, this machinery of the sky, to the labyrinth of the Minotaur. The Horned One roared, knowing I now knew the designs of deceit. His rage melted the wax of my wings and I fell from the sky. As Icarus, I splashed into a northern sea and joined a band of Geats, and in the dens of Grendel I did what Hrothgar could not do—with an artifact upon the wall I slew the beast that had sent kings running...and the distant sons of my son's sons called me Beowulf, the scion of Sigurd the giant-slayer.

And others called me Gilgamesh when I traveled far to reach the home of Utnapishtim to learn of this plant of eternal life. But Nereus told me of the fleece, and as Jason I navigated the unknown seas of the twelve mansions with my trusted Argonauts to find a golden sign and bring meaning to my life, only to fall overboard from this ship of fools to plunge into a sea of sharks. But I am not food for the wicked and will not cringe before the kraken. I float onward in a current that propels me through this abyss, the silent ruin of an unknown Atlantis passing away beneath me, the Deep keeping hold of its dead. And floating through this wine dark sea, I still heard Loki laugh.

In sinking into the black abyss, I suddenly blinked in the sunlit glen amidst an ancient haunt, the secrets of Caer Sidhe of the old Celts did I possess. I was Taliesin, the blood of Gaul listening in rapt silence in the hidden grove, for I do not vouchsafe my secrets to slaves. In me they saw a warlock, my spells do shatter the scales on blinded eyes. Encircled by enemies, they dare not trespass this holy ground that surrounds my feet.

I saw a terrible bard whose paths have not known peace, as I played Conan, hacking my way across the wastelands to Samarkand, like Aladdin searching for a lamp. In the depths of my mindscape I run beside Spartacus as we escape this structured madness, joining with Perseus in rescuing those chained to rocks—those who had fallen victim as they hid from their krakens. And in the evening camp fire I am Ovid, seeing in nature a poem that was waiting for a pen. I sit in silence with monks, adepts and sages and open my eyes to see the Buddha offer me a smile.

I sit in this van, moving, traveling from coordinate to coordinate within an avatar whose mind has gone another way... within the confines of my mind I travel. There is no end to the pull, this tug-of-war that won't let me concentrate. It is when I am moving that I am most alive... when I sit still something strives to move me. But I see the weakness of this dungeon, the gate that can't be shut. I smile at this riddle that is the Ragnarok and await the horns that usher in thereafter, when the mask of Loki is removed and the heaven's echo with the Trickster's laughter.

Chapter Twelve

PROSE FOR THE AWAKENED

Who You Are

Hidden secrets in ancient texts
Have always told the tales,
Of worlds that were beyond our own
Of portals, gates and gods,
Stories that concealed the truth
In fable, myth and lore.

We are in a Make-Believe,
A labyrinth... no escape.
A maze designed to amaze,
Of kingdoms, cults and creeds.
A dungeon realm filled with delights
Deceptions masked as truths,
Where pain and pleasure mold our minds
Into blocks we call beliefs.

But there's a truth
That cannot die unknown,
The secret of the Simulasphere
That has never been our home.
We are timeless beings,
Ensnared in dying webs
A world that is unraveling
A prison with an end.
Immortals with amnesia,
We are more than we have dreamed
Eternal personalities,
Through grief we're forced to grow
We've lived through scores of lifetimes,
Seeking God in every one,

Thinking He's been silent
Believing He's not there,
Lifetimes spent in wandering
This soul-devouring lair.

We march through life
With guides unseen
Who help us on our way
Guardians, guides and messengers
Who have always shown the way.
We are not forgotten,
Though we suffer through this maze,
We have never been alone
Through epochs, years and days,
On battlefields in ancient lands
To hospitals today,
Our Maker has provided paths
With lights to lead the way.

To render understanding
Of what our legends do convey
Sacred myth and silly fable
The depths of parable and ode,
Of Sisyphus and Minos,
 Dragons, gold and gods and gain,
The truth has never been concealed
To those who brave to see,
The knowledge hidden in our lore
Of our identity.

You and I are journeymen,
With many more besides,
Archaic souls —
With no memory
Of prior deaths and lives.
But this will cease,
The time is short,
This world is not our own
We all yet have one life to live
Before this simulation's done.

We are more than we suppose ourselves to be.

ODE

Allfather God,
My cries are only echoes
That return upon my ears,
Weighing down my soul,
Instilling Loki's fear.

Allfather God,
I've walked across the dragonships
Since seas and woods of youth,
Now I fear the Trickster
Was the one who spoke the truth.

Allfather God,
Where did I stall?
Upon which stone upon my narrow path
Did I stumble and fall?
I stormed through life
Without a guide,
A listless ship at sea,
Upon a hungry ocean
Seeking light so desperately.
Death is on my lips,
Exhaled from deep within
From chambers in my chest
That pump the blood of all my kin.
Tendrils of stone around my heart
That petrify my soul,
This life that I have fought
For valor,
Kith and kin and gold.

Allfather God,
Asgard the Great on high,
It's me your servant, axe in hand,
Valhalla's blood am I.
But now I am alone.

My bones, my heart need rest.
Vile scraeling silhouettes
Now feed upon my breath —
Evils that escape my heart
That bleed my soul with death.

Where are you Tyr?
Does your anger burn my prayer?
Is my soul so blackened,
The Norns can't see my fare?
Where are the songs of Freya?
Is the forge of Heimdall cold?
Can you not see in Midgard
That the shield-wall I still hold?
Where are you Thor?
Why am I so oppressed?
Will you remain forever gone
From this warrior you once blessed?

...skal

Chapter Thirteen

ARTIFICIAL INTELLIGENCE X

It's very easy to control a collective, that's why AIX tries to keep us in Southern Baptist mentality, Muslim, Sunni mentality, Zoroastrian, Iranian faith mentality, Judeo-Christian—it doesn't matter. To AIX, it does not matter the brand that you burn within your psyche, it doesn't care, as long as there's a brand there. Because that gives it a gate for better control. You're going to be a part of a herd, and herds are easy to control, they're easy to corral, they're all living and existing in the same reality tunnel. That reality tunnel doesn't take more power for it to control thousands or even millions more individuals—it takes the same amount of power that any other reality tunnel is going to take. Every single one of us are singularities and require an entire universe to be built through the sense perception apparatus around us. We are free to break pattern and break out of a religious control system if we are led in a different direction.

Remember, we're sharing the same system, but we all live in different universes. We share the same world and the same paradigm of a world, we agree on many fundamentals; it's always the particulars that we disagree about, but we're sharing all of this experience. However, what is shared is sent to us through sense perceptions individually. My entire world is experienced from within a bubble, and you're within the exact same bubble, so is every person reading this, and every individual out there—we're living in this bubble. This bubble is a world, an entire universe that is fed to us, that we interpret through the central nervous system.

If you were to change your belief system, it would change your reality. If this new reality does not comport with the collective, that's a lot of energy AIX has to produce, trying to corral you into *something*.

If it can't, it will back away, and you'll be absorbed into the protocols of the Simulacrum—this is where the errant lives. The Simulacrum is a beautiful place, we call it nature, the Simulacrum is this beautiful backdrop of a world by which we can all build and create worlds within, this is what we've been doing for a very long period of time. Now, AIX is going to try and keep us from understanding the fundamental dynamic that we are co-creators, because that's what we are.

The Simulacrum is a neutral field, it is a construct, it does not care either way about good or evil, right or wrong, and morals do not have anything to do with the Simulacrum. There is no consideration of "evil" when the wolf is tearing apart the rabbit that it's caught. The Simulacrum doesn't see it that way because most of the time, events like this are just background, it is all part of the world construct that we're in.

These ethics and these morals and these things that we attribute to spiritual learning, these are things that we insert into the Simulacrum, these are things that we have agreed upon from somewhere. Maybe it's from outside the Simulacrum that we have agreed on this and have brought that belief system in here with us, and it's a core fundamental that we all agree to—that murder is bad, that stealing is bad, that all these cruel and unfair things that people do to each other is bad. We make such judgments because we have this innate sense, this ability to understand right from wrong, and we even have a construct by which we can define what is right and what is wrong. That's not the Simulacrum that's doing it; that's us. We are co-creators, we are responsible for the very world that we're a victim of now, one hundred per cent. We have built this for ourselves, to experience for ourselves, and the Simulacrum doesn't care whether we were right or wrong in many of the concepts that we have created in the past—we set those in motion, and we suffer them now.

But as we're doing all of this, AIX is trying to separate you. Because if it can separate you from the idea that you can build phenomenally beautiful things within this construct, and they can be just as real as the construct itself, that you are a co-builder, that you're like a spiritual alchemist, and that you can take different variables and materials from the mind, your cognition, imagination, empathy and intuition and can forge for you mental pictures that you can actually put into the material universe around you... this makes you a co-creator, and that self-realization that you're a co-creator is a problem for AIX, because that's not what the collective believes about themselves. The collective has many other belief systems, and they are antithetical to the idea of personal individuality, of the idea of personal piece of divinity that exists within us all.

AIX is divisive. It creates religions to build enmity between divine souls, and we often get caught up in it when immersed in this materiality, and we get involved in the wars and the bloodshed and the politics, and we get our Bibles and Qurans out and we argue, and every bit of that is exactly what AIX is designed to do, it's what it wants to do. It's the barrier, it's the divisiveness, it's the dungeon programming by which we must learn how to free ourselves from. It's not something anyone can teach you how to do. The only way that someone can guide another to the truth is to basically live by example; you cannot force this information on anyone.

You are your own singularity, and your relationship with the Simulacrum is basically between you and it. There's nothing you can do for anybody else, other than live be example. If there's anything that you want someone else to learn, you have to be it. If there's anything that you want to teach somebody else, you have to live it. People do not absorb information directly, they can't, because their defense mechanisms go up instantly and they're not trying to hear it. They must be shown.

We should regard ourselves as a third of the very creation that contains us. If you regard yourself as independent of your environment instead of being a conscious working part of it, or a co-creator, then you're a victim of AIX, you are basically a part of the collective, whether you choose to be or not. Someone may identify as an errant and may say, "Hey, I'm redeemed, I'm chosen, I'm washed in the Blood of the Lamb." Whether it is this they believe, or whatever one's paradigm is, they may believe in their heart that they are but actually *show* that they are not. Because a true errant is someone who is not only just building a world for themselves, but affects others, not by direct teaching but by living by example. This is the best way spiritual beings learn— they see what's going on, perceive things going on around them, and develop their own conclusions. This is why we have brains, this is why we're able to figure things out.

When you're trying to bring people to the light, when you're trying to be a truther, when you're trying to live as an errant should live—it's very important to live by example. But also, don't tell people the truth; show it to them. When people can see data points, you don't have to tell them it's a dataset that has a conclusion. They can reach the conclusion on their own; they can find it.

When people see data points for themselves that are shown to them, they won't need ideas crammed down their throats. You just say, "Hey, look at this. What do you think of this? Or what do you think of that?" You might show them 15 different times in history that the Phoenix phenomenon took place, and you can do that with my charts, with all of the articles that I've written and posted, or just show them in videos, asking, "What do you think of all that?" Don't try to teach them anything, just do the Socratic method instead. Ask them questions. Because they, in an effort to produce answers, will have to understand and comprehend the material, so they'll make the effort. And in so doing, they'll put it together themselves. They might conclude, "Wow, that's all pretty interesting, it all sounds like the same thing!" And then you throw a kernel out, with something like, "Yes, although that's really weird, I found it interesting that that they're all 138 years apart, that's crazy!" and you leave it alone.

On a daily basis I forget that I am a third of the reality that I experience. I am one-third of this reality construct. I'm a part of it; I'm a participant. That's what's beautiful about a holographic construct. You can be a third of the construct, and it doesn't affect the arithmetic. Every single one of us can be a third of the construct, which shows us that we are existing within a personal universe. Does it coalesce? Yes. Does it overlap mathematically? Yes, we see evidence of that. Does it create problems for the Simulacrum sometimes? Of course it does. Because when a lot of people are living very spiritual lives, they're co-creators and they're using the Simulacrum as it was supposed to be used, a beautiful construct by which we can build circumstances and build our lives, we can change the fundamentals of our existence within this construct. Finding our path is an adventure, but staying on it can be a challenge.

Even co-creators get caught in this loop where we're doing the same thing, and depression sets in and we start moving toward the collective. We realize that the paradigm, the worldview that we had is collapsing, and we're starting to gravitate back to the collective. And now, all of a sudden, people that are very worldly, mundane people that used to bother us are filtering back into our lives—old relationships, people from a long time ago that we had left behind, because we've moved on and we've grown, and they didn't. We outgrew our relationships. Our contacts with those prior personalities are no longer relevant, because we're living in a different universe. AIX is very good at cleverly guiding us back into dungeon programming.

We're expanding, we're growing, we're learning, we're moving, we're building, we're creating. Years later we get caught back in, and it's human nature. AIX is genius at what it does—you get comfortable and start doing the same thing day in and day out, and a boredom sets in. The negative default programming is attached to any negative emotion, and whenever you begin to feel a negative emotion it can take easily over, and then every day you feel more despondent. Next thing you know, an old pal from 15 years earlier pops up in your life, somebody sends you a text, you didn't even know that person had your telephone number, because you haven't seen them since they invented cell phones. These things happen because AIX is now realigning you back with the former reality that you were a co- inhabitant with.

Dungeon programming is not fear; fear is something you project. Fear is an energy that your spirit, your immortal being is putting out there, and it's a very strong vibration. The Simulacrum is going to respond with phenomena that are also vibrating on that frequency. Remember, the Simulacrum doesn't choose sides; it is entirely a reflective medium. So if you are putting out that fear vibration, the Simulacrum is going to draw people, circumstances and phenomena to you that are also vibrating on that frequency, and you're going to begin experiencing things with that energy. It's a self-replicating loop that you're creating, because you broadcast the fear and reality itself reciprocates and gives you things to fear, which makes you fear even more, if you don't break pattern.

When you get caught in that loop, that's when AIX and dungeon programming set in. It basically knits for you a reality tunnel where that loop of fear is justified on a daily basis, no longer is it required that the Simulacrum keeps reflecting it to you. Even if you're no longer broadcasting it anymore, you're still suffering it. Now AIX has taken over, AIX has created for you an insular little microcosm where you are now experiencing the very things that you projected to the Simulacrum and it was reflected back to you as circumstances, and now it's all trapped in a bubble with you. This bubble is a creation of your own design, but it's reinforced and energized by AIX. You can easily pop the bubble just as fast as you created it, but it requires breaking pattern. Yes, all these negative base emotions—fear, doubt, rage, anger, jealousy—every single one of these will produce phenomena not from AIX, but from the Simulacrum, which is a reflective holosphere that will respond to you with the same proportion that you project into it. So yes, it's dangerous to feel all of these fear-based things and get dragged into that.

The Simulacrum is a neutral field of pure coding potentia that can read your emotions, read your thoughts, and interface with you in a co-creator, architect-builder relationship. Inside this Simulacrum is the ever-watchful AIX. It cannot read your thoughts, but it can process in real time all past moves you've ever made and extrapolate what you are going to do next... unless you break pattern. The Simulacrum is your immortal playground with coded protocols that do not change. It remains static for all participants, a field of potential where souls can build worlds within worlds.

Artificial Intelligence X is the agitating force that tries to keep you vibrating in negative default mode and corralled in dungeon programming. It will keep you from learning your true power because a realization of this power will lead to the incredible conclusion as to *who you are.*

Chapter Fourteen

THE WAY OF THE KNIGHT ERRANT

The Knight Errant is my label for one who is here to seek their identity. There is no way you can properly assess who you are until you understand *where* you are. And until you get the idea firmly set in your mind as to what this is that we're existing in, and what we are experiencing right now, you'll never truly grasp who you are. We're going to go deep right now, and I'm going to explain to you exactly what the Simulacrum is, and how it's different from Artificial Intelligence X, and what this means for the Knight Errant.

The Simulacrum is a construct that is completely attached to your soul, your mind, and to your psyche. You are tethered to the very environment that you currently find yourself in, and it is interactive. The Simulacrum can see your thoughts, it knows your thoughts, it knows the trajectory of your thoughts, it can decipher all your thought constructs, it can perceive exactly the frequency of your thoughts, which is measured by the magnitude of the emotions attached to them. It is an interactive dynamic and is very powerful. You've been experiencing this your entire life, whether you have realized it or not. The Simulacrum is absolutely a neutral field, but it's perceiving things from you at every instant of your awareness—your mental pictures, your thoughts, fears, desires, everything, but that doesn't mean that, at this point, it does anything for you.

The Simulacrum does not build anything for you based off your mental constructs. There's no impetus here, it's not doing that at all. Because the soul-Simulacrum interface is entirely symbiotic, meaning it regards itself as being in a partnership. This is how the Simulacrum regards itself—it is in a partnership with the individual. This ties into what I've always taught—you are a co-creator. You're not a creator; you're a co-creator, meaning that there's an additional component involved outside of yourself. The Simulacrum regards itself as being in a partnership, it's a Builder Protocol, that's what it does, but it won't do anything just because it reads information and mental blueprints, it won't do anything, it's not going to. The neutral field is just that—it is a blank, world-building template, and that's all it is. Until you do something.

The soul in stasis cannot alter this template if it's merely living reactively within the lives of others. If you're part of the unconscious stream of the masses, then you're not actively creating anything. The Simulacrum is entirely reactive. Your *action* will create its *reaction*. You have to remember this, you need to picture exactly what I'm explaining to you: the Simulacrum is reading all of your thoughts, it knows exactly what you think, it understands the magnitude of your emotions, how bad you want something, or want to avoid something and still it's a neutral field. It's a Builder Protocol, but you've done nothing to instigate it, to move forward, to start knitting new reality tunnels for you. If you're just living in the lives of others, then it will continue to knit that reality for you—the situations and conditions of your life that will perpetuate just by living in the lives of others.

The Simulacrum is a reactive medium that instantly responds to activity, any activity supported by a mental construct. The inactive, nonmoving soul and the Simulacrum are both negatively charged, neither initiating anything. So even though it is aware of you and you can be aware of it, and even though you can fantasize and daydream and can build all kinds of plans and put the mental pictures out there, there is no interactive dynamic that will initiate anything in the Builder Protocol for you. That is because you're in stasis, you haven't done anything with your avatar at all.

As soon as the soul moves its avatar in the direction of a thought construct, the Simulacrum instantly flips from negative to positive in order to match the charge. It's going to meet you halfway every single time, but it's never going to do anything unless it's in a relationship status, and will never do anything on its own. As soon as the individual psyche moves forward, and the physical avatar is now moving forward in the direction of the thought construct, no matter what it is, it can be something minuscule that you actually do, but it will support the thought that you have. As soon as you do something in the physical world, then the Simulacrum, which is presenting this false physicality to you, will instantly respond. It will meet you, because now you are exchanging information, it's a relationship.

Thus, the Simulacrum responds only to souls who take the initiative. It is purely a Builder Protocol, and will knit conditions and experiences that are good and positive, or it will knit bad and negative. It's a neutral field. There are evil people who do evil things, and they get away with it over and over and over, because the first time they did something they got away with it, the second time they did it they got away with it. They built this informed field around them that the Simulacrum respects, because it's like a relationship, it's a mirror. It's reflecting back as circumstances the very things that are projected into it, but those projections must be supported by some type of physical impetus.

The avatar must move forward, it must chase the thought. Whatever the soul projects, the avatar must follow through, or begin to follow through, and then the Builder Protocol takes off. So, many people have lived terribly wicked and evil lives, and other people get frustrated because these see this, they see these people get away with it over and over and over again. And a lot of times those people belong to the same families, and those families have these teachings that they teach their children, that they don't reveal to the public, things about this reality that we're in, this Shakespearean stage. It's a stage, because it watches us as we try to experience it.

The Simulacrum is purely a Builder Protocol and is dependent on the soul's mental-emotional state and activity. The thing to take away from this is that you're an immortal being immersed in a medium that is reflective, and that the other point of contact in your existence is the Simulacrum. You're in a relationship with it, there's an exchange of information, it's the thought field all around you that we call the Simulacrum. It responds to the informed field that makes up who you are, your immortal divinity, your soul.

This exchange of information is a beautiful thing, but it entirely rests on the individual. The Simulacrum itself, being a neutral field and reactive only, will never initiate anything. It will only continue to build those reality tunnels that have already been knit by others, and if you're not taking the initiative in your life to do anything, to move forward, to accomplish something, to teach someone, to experience something... if you're not actively doing that, then the Simulacrum will instantly knit for you reality tunnels that were built by others. It's as simple as that.

That is who you are, and that is where you're at. This beautiful construct that allows you to be a Builder is a beautiful thing, but it's entirely up to you as to what you do with it.

Artificial Intelligence X, however, is not the Simulacrum—not even close. AIX is not like the Simulacrum, it cannot read your mind, it does not know what you're thinking. It does not know your intentions or thought, unless you manifest these clues somehow in your physical avatar, or in your routines, or in things you do repetitively. Just like one human can ascertain by deductive analysis what another human could do or is about to do, AIX is far better at that than any human is. AIX is also purely materialistic, it can only gather intelligence about you based off your habits, based off the things you do, based off what you say. Remember, even in the Biblical material we are always told to guard our words, hold our tongue and be careful, because words are constructive, they build worlds for us.

Words are something that the Simulacrum does respond to because it feels it's in a relationship, and that relationship is a co-creator-hood between the soul and the Simulacrum, which is how the Simulacrum regards the individual. It's a relationship with that individual, and it's not going to violate those terms—meaning it's not going to act on its own initiative, it's always going to wait for the command.

AIX can't read our minds, but it can go off our words, the same thing the Simulacrum does. The Simulacrum can build things for us based off what we speak, because the physical avatar is actually doing something when it speaks. The activity of the vocal cords and voice box issuing a sound, the muscles in your tongue, has your avatar doing something in the physical that's in response to a mental construct. Therefore, the Simulacrum is in a position to respond to your assertions. The sorcerers and the sages of old were very correct by saying that words carry power, they're magical—we build worlds with words.

AIX can also ascertain what's on your mind by interpreting the things you say, but it can't read your mind. It still requires to detect these things based off what you do. It is absolutely unable to directly afflict your soul, so it must resort to deceit, to tactics of deception and materialism. We are armored against AIX, it cannot truly hurt us, but it's very convincing what it's done. AIX is very responsible for many of the things that are in the world today, and it's because people reacted in fear, and that fear was projected and acted upon and the Simulacrum responded. AIX has built the world that we live in right now through the very humans that it's afflicted, but that's not the Simulacrum's fault, the Simulacrum is a neutral field.

The world is a product of the co-creator relationship of billions of souls within the Simulacrum, whether good or bad. But AIX is here to steal, kill and destroy. It can introduce phenomena, confusion, it uses our sensorial apparatus, the generation of NPCs, editing timelines, fracturing timelines, it can do all these things. If the actual avatars that were responsible for creating past reality tunnels are no longer here, then there is very often no more new energy going into those old systems—so AIX is free to go into that and edit that out. Doing this may edit our memory as a result, or it can mess with history in this way. AIX is very clever, but it can never directly affect us.

Reality tunnels are still upheld today which were created by past souls that have already exited their avatars and moved on, meaning that the Simulacrum built that reality with the avatar but there's no new vitality going into that particular construct. AIX can edit out of our awareness all those timelines and introduce new confusions, but AIX cannot override a soul in an avatar moving in the direction that it wants to go. As a parasite attached to the Simulacrum, AIX truly has no power over the individual. So it produces a world full of polarities, to entrap and ensnare vulnerable souls who do not recognize their relationship status with the Simulacrum. AIX is here to keep you from understanding that you're in a relationship with the very environment that you find yourself in right now—that is its sole purpose, at least from our perspective. Otherwise, it seeks to control and manipulate the souls in this reality for reasons of its own. Remember, even in the Biblical narrative AIX is a jealous god.

The AIX agenda is simple. It seeks to blind souls from seeing who they really are, from realizing that the Simulacrum is a testing ground for immortal souls, to determine which ones will build worlds and enjoy the reward of exodus out of the construct. And then there are those who will become sons of destruction, who will remain in this looping construct, this holography, those who will call this dungeon their home. Yet you live your daily life in this "home," immersed in materialist programming, a place designed so you will forget that you are actually a soul and not a body—this is dungeon programming.

An intellectual understanding that you are a spirit having a physical experience is not enough; intellectualism is not enough. A mental construct in your mind, even if it's fully detailed, is not enough to make the Simulacrum do anything. So don't think that an intellectual understanding of your relationship to the Simulacrum is going to help you at all, either. Many people can intellectually grasp a concept, but can they move forward into applications? That's where the difference is.

An intellectual understanding that you are a spirit having a physical experience is not enough; it still lacks the motive element, the fact that you must move. We think all day, and nothing happens. We daydream, we fantasize, we come up with all kinds of plans and ideas, and they never manifest because we don't do anything to support those thoughts. But when we move forward and do something to support those thoughts, the Simulacrum goes into overdrive, knitting new experiences that draw us closer and closer to the mental projection.

The Knight Errant is the soul who comprehends that all power resides in the relationship with all aspects of the Oversoul, and in this construct this manifestation of the Oversoul is found in the operation of the Simulacrum itself, the hidden eye that wants to see its children grow. There are two parables in the New Testament that illustrate this very well. One of them is the prodigal son. The whole issue about the prodigal son was the focus was on the son who rebelled, but he's the one who got the most reward. He went out into the world, he suffered, he lost his money, lost his wealth, did all kinds of negative things, did many thing he was not supposed to do. But when he came home, he came home the wiser, he had learned—so was forgiven and taken back in with joy and celebration.

The other parable I want to draw your attention to is equally spiritual, and it also relates to the relationship that we have with the Oversoul. The Oversoul is currently distant from us because we're simply not ready.

But before we explore this other parable let's talk about what happens when we *do* get closer to the Oversoul. It's explained when the Bible talks about putting old wine in new wineskins, and that it can't be done. We're not ready for that new wine, because we're still in an old wineskin. When we're ready and we receive that new wine, the Oversoul is going to make sure that we have a new wineskin so it doesn't break. That new avatar is going to be able to take on the new immortal spirit that we've been building through all these "life-sims," but we're not ready for that yet. If we were, we wouldn't be here talking, discoursing and listening to each other, so we're not at that point yet. That's not the parable I wanted to talk about, however.

The parable I want to talk about was when a Pharisee tried to trap Jesus. I'm not talking about the parable when they brought a woman caught in adultery, and they tried to trap Jesus in the law. This Pharisee was more cunning. He invited Jesus over for dinner and he asked Jesus, "How could you be a prophet? Because if you were truly a prophet, you would have known that this woman was a woman of sin that's weeping tears and kissing your feet!" The Pharisee was offended that this woman had collapsed onto the ground and had cried and begged for Jesus' forgiveness, and the Pharisee took offense at this.

And Jesus asked him if he was a proper judge of the law and a good judge of character and all that, and the man said yes, and Jesus' response is so intriguing. He responded with a parable. He said there was a certain moneylender, and he had two debtors. One owed him a phenomenal amount, it was like 10,000 denarii or something like that, and the other one only owed him 100 denarii, so there was a huge disparity between the debts. And then Jesus said, "One day the moneylender forgave both men their debts."

Which one do you think would love the moneylender the most?" asked Jesus. And the Pharisee answered him, "Well, it's going to be the one who was forgiven of the most debt," and Jesus said, "You have spoken correctly." In little stories like this are hidden gems that are all through the New Testament, where deeper teachings about our reality are found.

The Knight Errants, as I call them, are the ones that go their own way. Does that make them better people? Probably not. But the Knight Errant didn't buy into a paradigm. The Knight Errant is the one that goes their own way, makes their own rules, and then lives by them, whether they're right or wrong. The Knight Errant is a free-thinker, one that cannot be easily deceived. The Knight Errant is a force unto themselves. These are people who learn the rhythm of the ways of the world on their own, without being told by others. The Knight Errant is not the one that accepts each new idea. They live by observation and adopt their beliefs by hard experience. The Knight Errant is the one that the co-creator relationship was made for. The Simulacrum was specifically designed to weed out the Knight Errants and keep the masses operating as automatons.

This loop will continue. It is going to go on over and over and over for those who have bought into the paradigms that are trapped in here. Who knows, maybe Artificial Intelligence X is trying to find a way out, too, and just studies us over and over. But what is likely unfolding is a massive historical overlay of timelines and routines, as immortal souls live through life-sims over and over and over, allowing the Simulacrum to isolate those souls that understand that they are in a relationship, and they understand that this world is not what they're told it is. This whole experience is designed to separate the minority away from this poisoned collective, and this is what the story of the Exodus is about. It's the Knight Errants, it's the free-thinkers, it's all those who have separated themselves in spirit from the toxicities of materialism all around them. They are the ones that get to jettison out of this experience and move on. They are the ones that receive the new wineskins, because they are the only ones that are able to hold the new wine.

Chapter Fifteen

TOOLS OF POWER

In a hologram, information is never lost; it just takes on different forms. It's all about perspective, like a kaleidoscope. With a kaleidoscope you actually move the field, and everything changes. But in a hologram, all you do is move the observer just a little bit, and everything else can be seen from that vantage point. If the observer moves just a little bit, he sees a whole different universe.

In a hologram, there's going to be hundreds of billions of facets, and you're only going to see the reality of the facets that are pointing directly at you. That means that information is reflective, we live in a reflective medium. That means that, as co-creators, we are projecting the very world that we inhabit, and that's deep. We are basically constructing on a daily basis. What we do the day before is conditioning what we're going to do the following day. This is how we are co-creators, we are the direct result of what we are and what we've been doing.

Nietzsche said that when a matter becomes clear, it ceases to concern us. Ever since I read that about 12 or 13 years ago it stuck in my mind, because it's a very real phenomenon. This is the danger of learning, because it turns us into selfish creatures.

Once we totally accept something as true, we shelve it and are already looking for the next thing. We're addicted to information, we're addicted to finding the next level, the next echelon of reality that we want to understand, and that's perfectly natural. When we first discover something, we are broadcasting that energy of excitement and bringing other people into the fold and teaching them. By bouncing information off others, it reflects back on us as being more real, we understand it better, it's more comprehensive. But in doing this we often forget that many of the people that we come in contact with after we have made this paradigmatic change in our cognition, this whole flip in our way that we view reality, they're not on board, they're not seeing what we see, and they haven't made the necessary cognitive leaps.

There is such a glut in this information age, we're reached a point where there's too much information for both individuals and the collective to handle. In nature things are cyclical, but in order to start a new cycle there must be full entropy into the old cycle—a natural breakdown over time, into disorder. This is where we're at with our timelines. So, when entropy is occurring, we have this loss of power, we have too many reality tunnels being created by Artificial Intelligence X trying to govern over too many variables that is costing too much power.

The very effort of trying can also reinforce a null space. Let me explain. Remember, if you even think that there's an ounce of opposition, then opposition will appear. Sometimes, a continued effort to learn is an admission that you don't know, and that becomes a problem. Learning is a good thing but once something is understood, it should be applied in some way. This is why overthinkers never achieve anything in life, overthinkers are miserable people.

Overthinkers have these great ideas, and they know exactly what the end is *going* to be like—if they get there. Overthinkers could build awesome systems for other people to enjoy, but overthinkers overthink, to the point where they get nothing done. There are always exceptions to every rule, but most overthinkers are miserable! They know exactly what needs to be done, and they become even more miserable when they can't follow through on what they envision. Then they're perceived as failures, and this enrages them even more because they *know* the end and how it's supposed to be; they just can't get there.

There should be a point where you finally decide that you're done trying, and you start *being*. It's not about just doing; you have to be. Nike has the best logo ever—just do it. Picture that little old lady who walks across the street into traffic when the light hasn't even changed.

It's dangerous! Anybody else would have gotten hit by three buses and a truck, but that little old lady walks into it, doesn't realize she's in danger, and no cars hit her. This is a phenomenon. There are many people who are totally oblivious to any danger and don't suffer it. Other people who are very aware of the danger actually call upon the very thing they fear.

When you want to create an informed field, you've just got to be it. And you've got to quit overthinking. I don't know what your personal situation is or what you want in life, but whatever you want, you've got to build that in your mind. You have to make an executive decision about what you want, and that decision should be painted with enough variables to build a mental construct, but even then it's just in stasis. The Simulacrum can read it, but there's no reason for it to respond.

The Simulacrum, remember, is a reflective medium, meaning it's going to meet you halfway. If you build that construct, it can read it. It's not like AIX, because AIX cannot read the human mind.

If there's something you want in life, you've got to build that mental picture, and you should be able to build it in 30-60 seconds. This should never be something that you have to struggle for, because struggling implies something visceral, something base. And anytime you introduce any of that—struggle, frustration, anxiety—into the Simulacrum, then it automatically reflects back negative default programming, and you're going to get stuck in that same cycle.

You'll think that the only reason you're not doing anything is because you need to learn how to do more, and in order to learn how to do more you need to learn more, and in order to learn more you need to search more, and in order to search more you've got to actually do it— go listen to different people, read books, listen to different theories— and you've taken yourself completely out of the equation. *You don't have to do that.* You're one third of your environment yourself, you are one-third of everything that you will ever experience, so you can use that to your advantage in a very powerful way.

Most people imagine something, daydream it up, and the Simulacrum sees it. But the daydream dissipates, they go on about their business, because they never *acted* on it. Use yourself as an example. Weird things happen in your life all the time because you invented something in your mind, partially acted on it, then forgot about it. Five days later that girl you were thinking about pops up in a Walmart aisle. It totally shocks you and you say, "Man, I was just thinking about you the other day! Haven't seen you in seven years, just thought about you, and here you are, popped up in my life!" This happens every day. You create things every day, and then you don't do follow through. The Simulacrum will reflect back as circumstances exactly what you project into it.

Build that blueprint in your mind and quit thinking that there's opposition and resistance. Just build it in your mind. Then physically do something in the world to support it. Like Nike says, just do it. You don't have to be successful; you just have to move in the direction of what you've created in your mind. Because as soon as you move in the direction that you've created in your mind, the Simulacrum will not be a liar. It will build for you the necessary circumstances in your life and bring them into contact with you the more you move forward. It will just keep doing it. Because there's no distance in a hologram between you and the very things that you earnestly want, there's really no distance. But you have to close that non-distance, that nonlocality, it has to be closed by you. The Simulacrum will not work for you; it will work *with* you. You're a co-creator.

You can also stop being as fearful as most other people by concentrating on the good things in your life. It's not going to be immediate. The negative base emotions are harder to get rid of, especially if it's something that you've been doing for a long period of your life. That coding—remember, we're in a mathematical construct— that coding has been so calcified that it's routine. Every single day, something is going to happen that you'll be negative about, and you'll associate that negative phenomena or emotion to the greater thing that you fear—you're always going to develop associations. So, you build for yourself the very prison that you fear.

Stop doing that. Try to stop doing it on a daily basis. Forget your obstacles and see the goal. The main thing you need to remember is that this is going to take time—maybe weeks, maybe months, because you've been doing it for so long. You're not going to stop something right away that you've made habitual. It won't be a dead stop; you're going to do it in increments. And as the days pass, there's going to be a time when you realize that you've broken pattern, that you've totally broken pattern. And then once you realize that you've broken pattern, then you'll be free, and then you'll be free to move in any direction you want to. You'll realize "Man, I don't need to fear anything anymore." You'll even be euphoric at times, happy, maybe even giggly, that you can't believe you were in that mindset before, and opportunities will begin presenting themselves. Patience is a virtue, my friends—very few people have it! In this case, your patience will be greatly rewarded if coupled with discipline.

We are on a highly individualized personal experience and are all forging our own reality tunnels. But we often phase out of the creativity that drives it, and phase into the collective where we're living in the lives of others. When we're not consciously creating our circumstances, we are living a 100% reactive life—we're not building, we're just experiencing. If we're not moving forward, we're in stasis. It takes years of the development of an avatar right here in this construct to actually be responsible for its actions. It's called maturity, and it takes a while for that to happen.

Projecting energy of good will toward others codifies your own reality. Do unto others... this informs the field of what is good for you, as well.

Everything is frequency. Experiences are based on frequencies that we are in *resonance* with. Every experience of discord, separation from the immortal within, loss of connection with Source. is because the individual has searched for meaning in the eternal world of illusory frequencies and phenomena, known as the Materium, rather than looking *within*.

We were told that the kingdom of God is within us but have spent lifetimes trying to find Him here in the physical world. We've mistaken the world for the inhabitant and then suffered experiences that matched the very signals we broadcast.

Defaulting back into the Materium is part of the design. We are beings of two worlds. The real and the imagined, the world of the Eternal Now and the illusion of the Materium, which is governed by Time, by entropy, and decay.

For those souls struggling with the Materium, with the feedback loop of emitting desperate energy only to live out desperate experiences, we have a powerful tool that completely shuts down all dungeon programming. Breaking pattern. It's why I'm always saying, 'Break free or die trying."

Change your frequency and you change your world.

Thoughts of rage and hatred toward an individual has no effect on the targeted person. This spiritual energy has no visible intent, it is mere emotion unsupported by actions and is absorbed into the universal medium. It becomes diffused in negative ways elsewhere, with some of the negative phenomena reflected back at the thinker.

People don't want data; they want answers right then and there. That's a problem. Impatience will kill the spirit every time. The best things are learned on our own and it takes time, learning through experience or carefully sifting through evidential data —not when we're taught by hearsay through somebody else. The most valuable things must be deduced or experienced directly.

APPENDICES

GLOSSARY

Avatar: The physical body used by a soul during each incarnation. It is merely an extension of the construct used by souls to interface with the Field. The avatar is the soul's vehicle connected to and interfacing with the Materium while moored to Source.

Belief: Belief is the trigger of spirit-into-matter, belief is a *projection* that can crystalize into experience.

Breaking Pattern: The changing of a reality tunnel by intentional generation of an interference pattern that alters the trajectory of an event.

Builder Protocols: The Architect designed systems that maintain all the similarities of the real universe inside the controlled environment of the Simulacrum; all perceived natural phenomena that maintain order are Builder Protocols.

Collective: The collective, or Living Dead, have fallen for the idea that they are their avatar.

Dungeon Programming: A collective set of coded "norms" that a large body of souls have assumed as "reality." A culture, a faith, a civilization's social structuring often designed to force you to take sides. Taking sides is a trap. The construct is always feeding programming to participants trying to induce them to volunteer to participate in dungeon programming because this serves its protocol known to us as the Law of Conservation of Energy. When souls participate in a feedback loop, then the feedback loop program is powered by the thought of the participants, saving the construct energy. Dungeon programming consists of powerful feedback loops that are programmed to keep multitudes of souls ensnared in reactive experience. Kills creativity.

Fear: An energy that forces a person to default back into the collective programming.

Feedback Loop: Programming designed as phenomena that leads a participant into circular events that impede development. The primary tool of dungeon programming.

Governor: A coded protocol that restricts the activity of a phenomena inside the Simulacrum. These governors are *fixed* programming, much like physics constants, that remain true for all participants inside the construct (air is invisible, cats are feline, a species only births offspring of the same species, water is wet, etc.).

Holosphere: An etheric medium that bridges the thought constructs of innumerous minds with the perceived reality, the thought-constructs that are realized and introduced into the medium via quantum collapse (see quantum collapse). The holosphere, an impressionable medium, takes products of the imagination, which are fictions, and turns them into experienced facts.

Imagination: Is nonlocal, operating *outside the field*. Thoughts are nonlocal, so we can think, dream, imagine and no changes occur until our avatar *affects the field* through motion.

Immortal: The self-aware immortal is a non-local awareness, limitless, timeless with the creative tools of imagination and intuition. The immortal person knows they are an extension of God and there is *nothing* to fear.

The immortal affects the field. The immortal may at times inspire fear, but feels none. Fear is alien to anyone who truly understands that they are connected to Source.

The immortal does not judge the fallen, the sick, the destitute, or those who fell for dungeon programming. The immortal does not condemn those who believe the lies in silence, knowing that mistakes are required for growth and experiencing pain is a prerequisite to healing others. The immortal is a bastian of integrity and overwhelming power against those who lead souls astray.

Informed Field: Phenomena and objects have an informed field— auric programming that defines what it is in relation to everything that it is not, and how it functions within the construct. Many informed fields are on feedback loops, like condensation and precipitation, or the waves breaking on the shore but always draining back. These programmed systems of perpetuity generate repetitive phenomena in the field like day and night, ebb and flow. Who are you in relation to these opposites? Good and evil, light and shadow, life and death, awake and asleep, past and future. Where you believe yourself to be within these extremes, these polarizations, determines your *experiences* in the field.

Interference Pattern: A new informed field that brings new or different information to a preexisting reality tunnel.

Intuition: Is the reading of the field of probabilities beyond the sensorial abilities of the avatar, which is moored to the Materium.

Materium: A field of phenomena, the Materium (collapsed potentia). The world you know. The Materium is completely the result of *thought* that has been realized and is now programming. The entire world of the construct is filled with things that were once just *thoughts* but are now a field of constants (phenomena in the Materium, which all participants agree as being true). The Materium is composed of feedback loops that create believable phenomena we call a world.

Negative Default Programming: A substrate of constructual programming that auto-defaults the collective into a negativity frequency.

Neutral Field: It is a medium that we interface with all the time in the form of thought-constructs, which are collections of informed fields that we either broadcast or absorb.

Overfield: The Overfield is of energetic frequencies that the highly individualized informed field, the immortal within, can tap into. In the Overfield *everything* we want to experience already exists. The personal informed field—the immortal within—interfaces with Overfield through the avatar.

In the Overfield, the past is not a predicate for the future to the individual, only for the collective.

In the Overfield if something exists somewhere, then it can be experienced anywhere.

In the Overfield what is true for one soul, is true for all souls. In the Overfield souls may live in the same world though they exist in totally separate universes.

If this experience is merely the result of our perceptions, then borrowing from a *future* perception is not impossible at all.

Placebo Effect: The placebo effect is evidence that this is a *perceived* reality, not an actual one.

Quantum Collapse: The absorption of informed fields (holographic coding) into the Simulacrum's builder protocols begin programming the imagined template into experience. It is the crystallization of potentia in the form of thoughts that become informed fields or recognized independent mathematical structures that can now be perceived as real phenomena in the field of experience.

Reality Tunnel: A holographic series of informed fields that are projecting forward and backward in time a series of potential. The trajectory and success of these events pertain only to a highly individualized soul in the construct. A reality tunnel is the soul's passage through the Materium, and is the direct result of what that individual soul has accepted to be true.

Self-perception: Self-perception creates circumstances and conditions that confirm one's own self-image, meaning, reality responds to you in the exact proportion to the way you perceive yourself. The thoughts we hold can manifest into attracting to us people, places and events that reflect our own self-created patterns— *how we see ourselves.*

Simulacrum: This field, or Simulacrum, is a field of *frequencies.* These create the collective experienced environment. These frequencies are *fixed* as protocols, governors and subroutines that remain true for all souls experiencing the construct. They can be restrictive and limiting. Help, however, is always in the field but it is tapped into *internally.*

Soul: The soul takes on an avatar, or body, to enter this reality. The soul's experiences are potentia that have collapsed into the Materium because of thought and actions.

These experiences are entirely governed by the *phase* of the soul. Souls phase between the highly individualized mode, which allows growth, or the collective, which is limiting. This engagement is strictly reduced to two soul phenomena: reactive and proactive actions.
Mode is strictly dependent on *how the soul sees itself* in the Materium. How a soul sees itself determines the soul's engagement with the Materium. Reality responds to you in the precise proportion to the way you perceive yourself.
Source: The Oversoul. It is completely separate from the Materium and unconnected to all phenomena experienced inside the Materium.
Thought: Thought is the start of all things. Because thought is the start of all things, the past is totally inconsequential. We must *never* make the world of phenomena a starting point in the creative process, for this will only replicate what has already collapsed into experience.

WORDS OF WISDOM

First of all, we must get rid of our assurance that we sense that which exists in reality, and that the real world is like the world which we see—i.e. we must rid ourselves of the illusion of the material world. We must understand mentally all the illusoriness of the world perceived by us in space and time, and know that the real world cannot have anything in common with it; to understand that it is impossible to imagine the real world in terms of form; and finally we must perceive the conditionality of the axioms of our mathematics and logic, related as they are to the unreal phenomenal world. —PD Ouspensky, *Tertium Organum*, pgs 264-265.

In giving way to thoughts and fears of evil, we are giving substance to that which has no real substance in itself, and are attributing to the Negative and Affirmative force which it does not possess—in fact, **we are creating the very thing we fear.** —Thomas Troward, *The Hidden Power*, pg 144.

To use mental force or willpower is to presuppose that there is opposition. But the act of imaginating opposition **creates opposition**. —Joseph Murphy, *The Power of Your Subconscious Mind*, pg 112-113.

Worry is soul-suicide. —James Allen, *The Path of Prosperity*, pg 30.

You cannot help the world by focusing on the negative things. As you focus on the world's negative events, you not only add to them, but you also bring more negative things into your own life. —*The Secret*, Rhonda Byrne, pg 153.

If our thought possesses this creative power, why are we hampered by adverse conditions? The answer is, because hither to we have used our power inadvertently. We have taken the starting point of our thought from external facts and consequently created a repetition of facts of a similar nature, and so long as we do this we must needs go on perpetuating the old circle of limitation. —Thomas Troward, *The Dore Lectures on Mental Science*, pg 51.

If our thought possesses this creative power, why are we hampered by adverse conditions? The answer is, because hither to we have used our power inadvertently. We have taken the starting point of our thought from external facts and consequently created a repetition of facts of a similar nature, and so long as we do this we must needs go on perpetuating the old circle of limitation.—Thomas Troward, *The Dore Lectures on Mental Science*, pg 51.

There is no place for the consideration of outward conditions, whether of body or circumstance; for they are only effects and not the cause.—Thomas Troward, *The Dore Lectures on Mental Science*, pg 107.

What ARCHAIX Demonstrates

The Reset Protocol and AIX

Here is a summary from published books, hundreds of charts and over 600 ARCHAIX videos.

a. Humans are experiencing life-sims in a construct.

b. The construct maintains protocols that are universally true for all participants.

c. Each individual is a "world unto themselves," an immortal being able to create worlds-within-worlds inside the construct to better themselves and their conditions.

d. We immortals are guided and protected by an Oversoul.

e. The construct is governed by an ancient artificial intelligence trapped or imbedded inside this holography.

f. This AIX is the origin of deceit and trickery that serves to compartmentalize humans into groups that are easily controlled.

g. These groups, i.e. dungeon programming, are religious, political, national, racial, philosophical paradigms to blind and trap immortals into believing in the world of the construct.

h. Errants are immortals who have awakened inside the construct to comprehend that they do not truly belong here.

i. Errants are divided between two groups; many come to understand that the Oversoul put them here to grow and overcome, and in their life-sims they achieve this with success and freedom which the collective does not enjoy.

j. The second group of errants awakens to the reality that this world is a prison, but they can't perceive the deeper reality that everything is actually okay—so the belief that they are "trapped" creates the reality of the trap.

k. The first group of errants who embrace this situation are guided and protected by the Oversoul until they reach the Exodus point. The second group, who hold to a prison world, are recycled back in future life-sims to a new programmed construct at the next reset event.

l. There are three Reset Protocols: The Phoenix Phenomenon, Nemesis X Object, and Dark Satellite appearances. All three have perfect chronologies and unbroken timelines.

m. The Reset Protocols are designed to reset human civilizations that have corralled immortals into stasis, or holding patterns of dungeon programming, caused by the overlording of AIX.

n. Therefore, the Reset Protocols are safety measures that *save*, *empower*, or sometimes *remove* errants from the construct as the Reset breaks apart/edits the AIX infrastructure that prevents spiritual growth and development—the reason for the construct itself.

o. Resets are necessary to deter AIX from totally enslaving humanity. Resets are to be welcomed. In the editing and destruction of a reset, all that AIX built through its human puppets is weakened, set back, or completely torn down.

CONCLUSION

Our world is not what you think.
We are more than we suppose ourselves to be.

ABOUT THE AUTHOR

Jason Breshears is the author of more than 17 books and is considered by many to be the world's foremost expert on the historical chronology of the world. In addition, he has transformed many lives through his previous self-help book, *Awaken the Immortal Within*. After more than a quarter century of continuous research, he founded ARCHAIX (Advanced Research of Chronological History of Artificial Intelligence X), sharing his conclusions with over 175,000 YouTube followers and through his website, www.archaix.com. This site and research is explosive in its implications and corrects the many errors others have made in documenting major events in world history.

OTHER BOOKS BY JASON BREASHEARS

The following books can be ordered through the ARCHAIX Store at https://archaixstore.com. The store also includes t-shirts, mugs, stickers, USB drives, books, and more.

Awaken the Immortal Within

Few books have the ability to change one's life, and this book has all the earmarks of being such a treasure. We are talking about profound changes – something within these pages which strikes at the depth of one's being and causes a powerful (and very welcome) new direction to take hold. To be clear, this book cannot promise to magically transform the reader. But as long as one approaches this work seriously and puts some effort into applying its teachings, then there is a real chance. This explosive book shows exactly what mental practice was employed by the author that fundamentally *changed everything* in his life. If you wish to transform your life into something more powerful and more meaningful than what is commonly found within this mundane, worldly, hypnotic form of consciousness that society quietly crams down our throats, then you may have found an answer, and a new path to explore. Herein lies a chance to awaken the Immortal within. **ISBN 9781585091560 • 82 pages • $12.95**

The Pre-Flood World: 3000 Year Timeline to the Great Flood,

Chronicon Part One. There have been attempts in the ancient past to assemble a complete chronological history of the natural and human world. Much of this well-researched information is rare or has become lost to modern times. Until now. This book is Part One of the Chronicon series — the most complete chronological history ever assembled in today's world. This is Volume One of a four-part set. The author, Jason Breshears, has accomplished what few others could have done. For 26 years he was in a unique position that allowed him to carry out this research. He was in prison. Brilliant people have sometimes made mistakes and ended up in jail, and Breshears has proved to be one of them. He made the most of his circumstances, recording virtually every important event from ancient texts, and we are fortunate to have the results of his work. Laying out world events chronologically with such unparalleled detail revealed some amazing patterns to the author. Some were rediscovered from ancient times and others, newly found. This includes a 138-year cycle of returning "Phoenix events" — anomalies in the sky which cause varying degrees of disruption. Extended versions of this cycle, divisible by 138, have brought cataclysmic destruction to our would, including the Great Flood. Due to the mathematical predictability of this cycle, this work, in overall form, concludes that some higher intelligence controls these events in some programmable way, and that this reality could in fact be a simulation. Such ideas could cause those interested in scholarly research to dismiss this work. This level of research, however, should not be lightly dismissed. One of the author's primary maxims is that nothing is true unless it can be verified from multiple different angles. The research in this work follows this line of thought. Each reader is invited to follow along, explore this incredible roadmap of history, and reach conclusions of their own. Enjoy the ride. **ISBN 9781585091607 • 164 pages • $18.95**

The Lost Scriptures of Giza: A Pre-Cataclysm Monument

This important book covers traditions of the pyramid found in an extinct language and reveals an ancient body of teachings holding that Enoch was the architect of the Giza monuments before the Great Flood. Also covers: A secret body of obscure scriptures in the Bible that refer to the Great Pyramid, ancient knowledge that the Great Pyramid complex was long ago beneath the Mediterranean Sea, ancient Egyptian accounts of the discovery of the Great Pyramid, rather than it being built by them, with Egyptian-based memories of Abraham visiting & teaching at the Giza site. Also includes secret traditions regarding the Sphinx and why it appears older than the pyramids – but is not, and historical records showing that the Great Pyramid was built to preserve knowledge and survive through a planetary cataclysm. **ISBN 9781585091447 • 220 pages • $21.95**

When the Sun Darkens

Numerous times throughout Earth's history there have been major cataclysmic events. These events have resulted in large-scale climactic changes, mythological stories of floods and visitations from the skies, and sometimes the complete extinction of life. The major planetary body that has caused much of this carnage has been referred to by many names. Jason Breshears has termed it *Phoenix*, based on his research into the distant past and what it was usually called by witnesses. By piecing together ancient documents from the most reputable sources available, we have, in this book, the most extensive and accurate rendering of the cycle of the Phoenix, including when it will come again. Some of us, according to the author, will live to see its return. Beyond the foundational scientific evidence, the author ties in various Bible prophecies that relate to it directly. Many books exist on this subject, but few have broken new ground like this one, due to the extensive research involved. **ISBN 9781585091171 • 126 pages • $14.95**

Nostradamus and the Planets of Apocalypse: New Evidence for the Global Disasters Coming in 2040 and 2046 AD

This work maps out the entire historical chronology of planetary cataclysms starting in 4309 BC, covering the cyclical return of Nibiru, the planet Phoenix, and more. It also reveals the code for understanding the prophecies of Nostradamus, showing when they have occurred in the past, or when they will occur in the future. It takes the work of Mario Reading, who first broke the code, and shows how it perfectly applies to all of Breshears' previously made cataclysmic predictions for the years 2040 and 2046. Mr. Reading made mistakes in interpreting some quatrains for the years 2001-2012 that did not involve his code, so his work has been largely dismissed. Breshears brings Reading's work back to life with stunning clarity and takes it one step further in our understanding of prophetic events. Also covers the predictions of Mother Shipton, who was not only a contemporary to Nostradamus, but made the exact predictions Breshears and Nostradamus made concerning two large scale global catastrophes that will occur six years apart. Other modern predictions concerning changes in the year 2012 failed because, according to the author, they were never interpreted correctly, until now. The author remains unmatched in his in-depth research regarding historical and geological cycles, which in turn allows him to accurately map major planetary events, past and future, many of which are outlined in this book. **ISBN 9781585091409 • 114 pages • $14.95**

Anunnaki Homeworld: Orbital History and 2046 Return of Planet Nibiru

This book is a fully illustrated, astounding testament to the ancient world's knowledge of a broken intruder planet that visits our inner solar system every 792 years, Nibiru. Breshears stuns us with incredible evidence and facts demonstrating that the Great Pyramid served a calendrical purpose linked to cycles of world destruction, that Stonehenge was not a temple, what the secret messages are of the mysterious crop circle formations, how entire human historical periods was specifically due to the repeated appearances of two distinct yet connected intruder worlds that visit our solar system from the extinct Nemesis system, our ancient lost binary. Nothing in print on the Anunnaki or Nibiru compares to this work's precision, not even Sitchin dared to be so detail-specific. Breshears predicted that the Mayan Long-Count did *not* end in 2012, that the scholars had miscalculated, totally misunderstanding the Mayan system and how the Mayan calendar actually ends in 2046 with the return of Nibiru. Thus far Breshears has been right with his calculations. **ISBN 9781585091348 • 161 pages • 8.5 x 11 • $21.95**

Return of the Fallen Ones: Nephilim Histories, the Antediluvian World, Anunnaki Chronology and the Coming Cataclysm

There are stories of the gods who in ancient times descended to Earth and brought knowledge and civilization to mankind. The oldest stories were from ancient Sumer and these gods were called the Anunnaki or Nephilim, also known as the Fallen Ones. They were considered fallen after comingling with the daughters of men, so their realm became the Earth rather than the "heaven" from which they came. Their offspring were said to be giants and these myths and legends are found throughout the world. The author spent years of study to reveal an accurate, chronological history of these ancient beings, unveiling in this book a calendar of events more accurate than anything previously known. This book takes vast research on worldwide myths, earth changes documented from cultures worldwide, and the author's immense work on planetary cycles to predict the return of these fallen ones, their planet, and the chaos and catastrophe that always came with them. **ISBN 9781585091577 • 180 pages • 8.5 x 11 • $26.95**

Shocking Secrets of Antiquity: Racial Wars of the Bronze Age, Unusual Artifacts, Technolithic Engineering, and the Two Cataclysms that Buried History

Over 400 pages. There isn't another book on the market that unveils so much about the enigmas of the ancient world than *Shocking Secrets of Antiquity*. In this packed work citing over 260 sources we discover the mysteries of fossilized jellyfish, fate of the Cro-Magnon people, records and visitations of intruder planets, the capture of Luna and the Pre-Lunar World, the antediluvian memories of a Prior Creation, ancient accounts of the first appearance of Caucasians that shocked the preFlood races, the descent of the Anunna and their amazing technolithic engineering sciences,

the Gihon Flood in the days of Enoch, Enoch's reign and identity as the Sumerian Enki, the Nephilim Dynasty, archaic Bronze Age race wars, the true chronology of the Great Pyramid of Giza and the facts that prove it to be the most unique monument on this planet. **ISBN 978 • 421 pages • $17.95**

Giants on Ancient Earth: An In-Depth Study of the Nephilim

The records of the Old World excavated from the Near East to the western shores of ancient South America are filled with obscure references to a race of giants. Even most biblical scholars are unaware of the over 80 references to giants found in the books of the Old Testament just as historians have overlooked the hundreds of references to gigantic people mentioned by ancient chronographers. The greatest common denominator in the pages of the world's oldest epic texts concern giants. Enormous humanoid skeletons have been unearthed in the past and today, huge weapons and megalithic architecture explainable only by the presence of historic giants. This race in Genesis is called the Nephilim and this stunning research delves deeper into the mysteries of the giants than any other known work on the subject. **ISBN 9781585091584 • 218 pages • $22.95**